Easy Word 7 for Windows® 95

Trudi Reisner

Easy Word 7 for Windows 95

Copyright © 1995 by Que® Corporation.

Library of Congress Catalog Card Number: 95-71076

International Standard Book Number: 0-7897-0081-6

98   8   7   6   5   4   3

Interpretation of the printing code: the rightmost double-digit number is the year of the book's first printing; the rightmost single-digit number is the number of the book's printing. For example, a printing code of 95-1 shows that this copy of the book was printed during the first printing of the book in 1995.

Screen reproductions in this book were created by means of the program Collage Plus from Inner Media, Inc., Hollis, NH.

This book was produced digitally by Macmillan Computer Publishing and manufactured using 100% computer-to-plate technology (filmless process), by Shepard Poorman Communications Corporation, Indianapolis, Indiana.

Credits

Publisher
Roland Elgey

Vice President and Publisher
Marie Butler-Knight

Publishing Manager
Barry Pruett

Editorial Services Director
Elizabeth Keaffaber

Managing Editor
Michael Cunningham

Product Development Manager
Faithe Wempen

Production Editors
Phil Kitchel
Audra Gable

Copy Editor
Silvette Pope

Technical Editor
June Waldman

Book Designers
Barbara Kordesh
Amy Peppler-Adams

Cover Designers
Dan Armstrong
Kim Scott

Indexer
Carol Sheehan

Production Team
Claudia Bell, Amy Cornwell, Anne
Dickerson, Damon Jordan, Bob
LaRoche Kaylene Riemen, Mike
Thomas

Illustration
Becky Beheler, Jason Hand, Clint
Lahnen, Laura Robbins, Craig Small,
Todd Wente

Composed in *Stone Serif* and *MCPdigital* by Que Corporation

About the Author

Trudi Reisner is a computer consultant specializing in training users of IBM PCs, PC-compatibles, and Apple Macintoshes in the use of applications software. She is the owner of Computer Training Solutions, a Boston, Massachusetts company that offers training, technical writing, curriculum development, and consulting services in software programs.

Trademark Acknowledgments

Contents

Introduction

What You Can Do with Word

Microsoft Word for Windows is one of the world's most popular word processing software programs. You could create your documents on a typewriter, but Word makes writing, editing, and printing easier.

Specifically, you can use Word to perform these functions:

- *Correct errors.* With a typewriter, after you press a key, that letter is committed to paper. To correct a mistake, you either have to amend the document—with stuff like *White-Out*—or retype it. With Word, you see the text on-screen. You can easily correct any typographical errors before you print the document.

- *Move around quickly.* With the document on-screen, you can move from one sentence, paragraph, or page to another. You can move quickly from the top of the document to the bottom and vice versa.

- *Make editing changes.* You can insert text into any location in your document. You can also quickly delete any amount of printed matter, ranging from a character to a whole block of text.

- *Rearrange your text.* When you sit down to write, you don't always write in order from the introduction to the summary. Ideas may occur to you in a different order. As you're writing the summary, you might think of an idea that belongs in the introduction. With Word, you can easily move and copy text from one location to another.

- *Restore deleted text.* When you accidentally delete text that you want to keep, you don't have to retype it. Instead, you can just restore the text.

- *Check spelling.* As you type, Word checks your document for misspellings and double words. If you're a poor typist, this feature enables you to concentrate on your writing and leave spelling errors for Word to catch.

■ *Search for text.* You can search your document for a particular word or phrase. For example, you can move quickly to the section of your document that discusses expenditures by searching for the word *expenditures*.

■ *Search and replace text.* You can quickly and easily make text replacements throughout the document. For example, you can change all occurrences of the name *Smith* to *Smythe* in a document.

■ *Make formatting changes.* Word enables you to change margins, tabs, and other formatting options easily. You can experiment with the settings until the document appears the way that you want it. Then you can print it.

■ *Change the appearance of your printed text.* You can bold, italicize, and underline text. Also, depending on your printer, you can use a different typeface.

■ *Preview your document.* You can preview your document to see how it will look when you print it. If you want to make changes before you print, you can do this when you return to normal view.

■ *Add bulleted lists.* Add bullets to your document to emphasize text. Word provides a range of bullets to meet your preferences or needs.

■ *Add borders.* Borders can be added to any text, paragraph, or document. They can be created in a variety of widths—from thin to thick. There is also a 3-D effect available for adding special effects.

■ *Create headers and footers.* Word offers the capability to create custom headers and footers for your documents, or you can choose from the standard selections that are offered.

■ *Import data or graphics into your document.* You can import graphics or data from other applications into your document.

■ *Create standardized documents.* You can use templates and wizards to create standardized and customized documents.

Task Sections

The Task sections include numbered steps that tell you how to accomplish certain tasks, such as saving a document or indenting a paragraph. The numbered steps walk you through a specific example so that you can learn the task by actually doing it.

Big Screen

At the beginning of each task is a large screen that shows how the computer screen will look at some key point in the task. Sometimes this will show what the screen looks like when you are finished. Other times, it will be an important step along the way.

TASK 1

Starting and Exiting Word for Windows

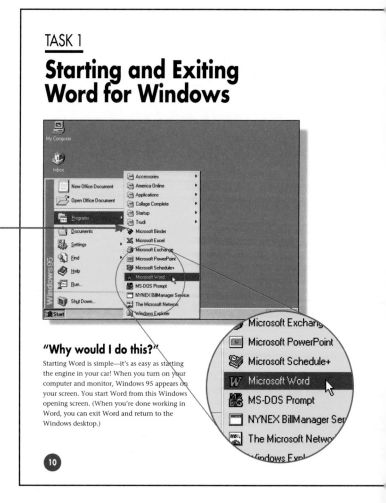

"Why would I do this?"

Starting Word is simple—it's as easy as starting the engine in your car! When you turn on your computer and monitor, Windows 95 appears on your screen. You start Word from this Windows opening screen. (When you're done working in Word, you can exit Word and return to the Windows desktop.)

10

Step-by-Step Screens

Each task includes a screen shot for each numbered step of a procedure. The screen shot shows how the computer screen looks at that particular step in the process.

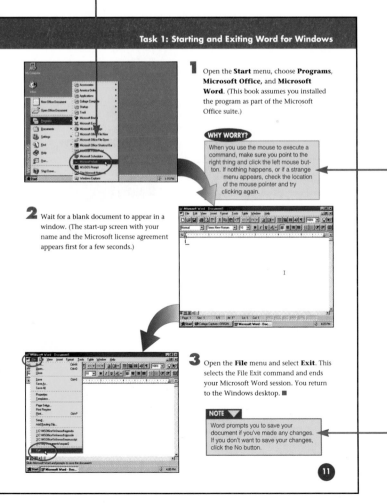

Task 1: Starting and Exiting Word for Windows

1 Open the **Start** menu, choose **Programs**, **Microsoft Office,** and **Microsoft Word**. (This book assumes you installed the program as part of the Microsoft Office suite.)

WHY WORRY?

When you use the mouse to execute a command, make sure you point to the right thing and click the left mouse button. If nothing happens, or if a strange menu appears, check the location of the mouse pointer and try clicking again.

2 Wait for a blank document to appear in a window. (The start-up screen with your name and the Microsoft license agreement appears first for a few seconds.)

3 Open the **File** menu and select **Exit**. This selects the File Exit command and ends your Microsoft Word session. You return to the Windows desktop. ■

NOTE ▼

Word prompts you to save your document if you've made any changes. If you don't want to save your changes, click the No button.

Why Worry? Notes

You may find that you performed a task (such as italicizing text following the numbered steps) correctly, but that the results didn't turn out the way you expected. The Why Worry? notes tell you about common problems you can expect or how to proceed if something doesn't work as planned.

Notes

Many tasks include Notes that tell you a little more about a procedure or alert you to a time-saving shortcut.

PART I

Getting Acquainted with the Word Screen

Microsoft Word is the top-selling word processing program in the world. You can use it to create professional-looking letters, reports, tables, memos, flyers, and much more. You can create almost anything that involves text in Word.

You can buy Word for Windows 95 as a stand-alone product or as part of a suite of programs called Microsoft Office. Office contains Word and several other programs that complement one another, such as a spreadsheet and a presentation program.

Before you can start Word, you must install it on your hard disk. (If Word is installed, it appears in your Windows Programs menu.) The exact procedure for installation depends on whether you purchased the CD or diskette version of the program, and whether you bought it as part of the Microsoft Office suite or as a separate program. For installation instructions, refer to your Microsoft Word Version 7 for Windows documentation.

In Part I, you'll learn how to start and exit Word. You can start and exit Word as you would any Windows application by selecting it from the Start menu.

Part I of this book also introduces you to the Word screen. When you start the program, Word displays a blank document—much like a blank piece of paper. The document is a file in which you store your data. The *insertion point* is a flashing vertical bar that appears in the document window. Text that you type appears at the position of the insertion point.

In this part, you learn how to view ToolTips (the toolbar button names). Word's ToolTips feature displays the button names for each button on the toolbar as well as a description of the button in the status bar.

This part also discusses some of the ways you can get help in Word. You can get instant online help, look at the Answer Wizard, and view the tip of the day. Word's tip of the day feature has tips for many Word operations.

For you to run Word for Windows 95, your computer must meet certain minimum requirements. You need to have Windows 95 running on your computer. The computer needs at least 4 MB of RAM and at least 9 MB of free space on the hard drive. (You'll be much better off if you have more RAM and more free disk space.)

If you have any questions about Word, you can contact Microsoft Word 7 technical support at (206) 635-7110.

To work most efficiently in Word, you should use a mouse. You press the mouse buttons and move the mouse in the following ways to change the way it acts.

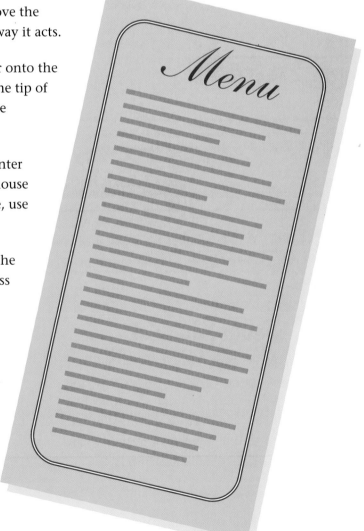

Point means to move the mouse pointer onto the specified item by moving the mouse. The tip of the mouse pointer must be touching the specified item.

Click on an item means to move the pointer onto the specified item and press the mouse button once. Unless specified otherwise, use the left mouse button.

Double-click on an item means to move the pointer onto the specified item and press the left mouse button twice quickly.

Drag means to move the mouse pointer onto the specified item, press and hold down the left mouse button, and move the mouse while holding down the button.

The tasks in this part teach you the skills you'll need to perform many of Word's operations.

Starting and Exiting Word for Windows

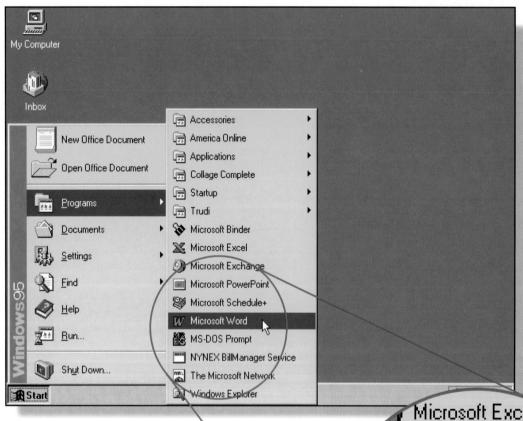

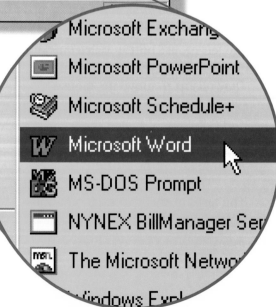

"Why would I do this?"

Starting Word is simple—it's as easy as starting the engine in your car! When you turn on your computer and monitor, Windows 95 appears on your screen. You start Word from this Windows opening screen. (When you're done working in Word, you can exit Word and return to the Windows desktop.)

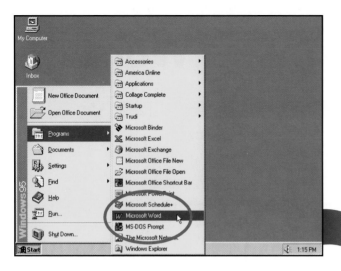

1 Open the **Start** menu, choose **Programs**, **Microsoft Office,** and **Microsoft Word**. (This book assumes you installed the program as part of the Microsoft Office suite.)

WHY WORRY?

When you use the mouse to execute a command, make sure you point to the right thing and click the left mouse button. If nothing happens, or if a strange menu appears, check the location of the mouse pointer and try clicking again.

2 Wait for a blank document to appear in a window. (The start-up screen with your name and the Microsoft license agreement appears first for a few seconds.)

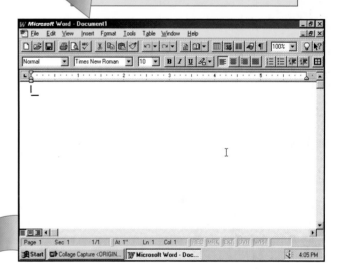

3 Open the **File** menu and select **Exit**. This selects the File Exit command and ends your Microsoft Word session. You return to the Windows desktop. ■

NOTE ▼

Word prompts you to save your document if you've made any changes. If you don't want to save your changes, click the No button.

TASK 2
Seeing What's New in Word

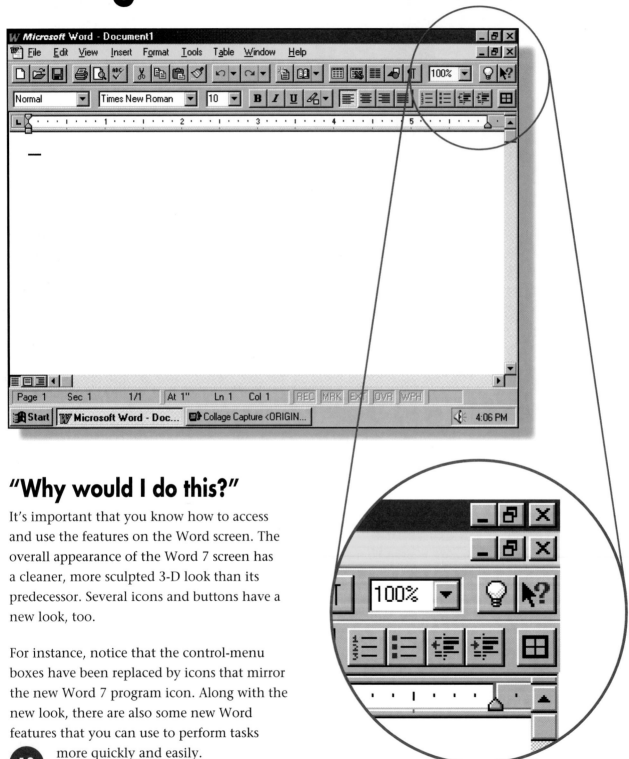

"Why would I do this?"

It's important that you know how to access and use the features on the Word screen. The overall appearance of the Word 7 screen has a cleaner, more sculpted 3-D look than its predecessor. Several icons and buttons have a new look, too.

For instance, notice that the control-menu boxes have been replaced by icons that mirror the new Word 7 program icon. Along with the new look, there are also some new Word features that you can use to perform tasks more quickly and easily.

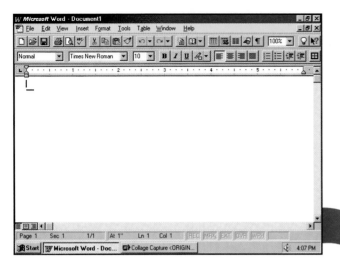

1 If you haven't started Word yet, start it now. If you need help with this step, see Task 1, "Starting and Exiting Word for Windows." You should see the Windows opening screen.

2 Click the application window's **Minimize** button (the button with the underscore) in the upper-right corner of the application window. The Word window becomes a button on the Windows taskbar at the bottom of the screen.

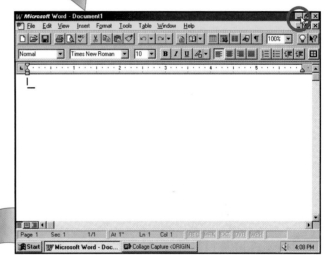

3 Click the **Microsoft Word** button on the taskbar to return to the Word application window.

4 Click the document window's **Minimize** button (the button that contains an underscore) near the right end of the menu bar. The document becomes a button above the Windows taskbar.

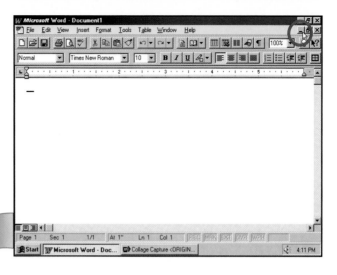

5 Click the **Maximize** button (the button that contains a full-size window) on the document button. Word enlarges the document window to full size.

NOTE ▼

To restore the application or document window to its previous size, click the application or document window's Restore button (the button that contains two windows).

6 Click the **Close (X)** button in the upper-right corner of the document window. Word closes the document window. ■

NOTE ▼

To close the application window and exit Word, click the Close (X) button in the upper-right corner of the application window.

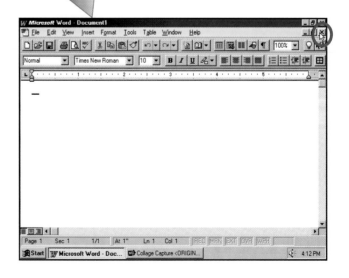

Selecting a Menu Command

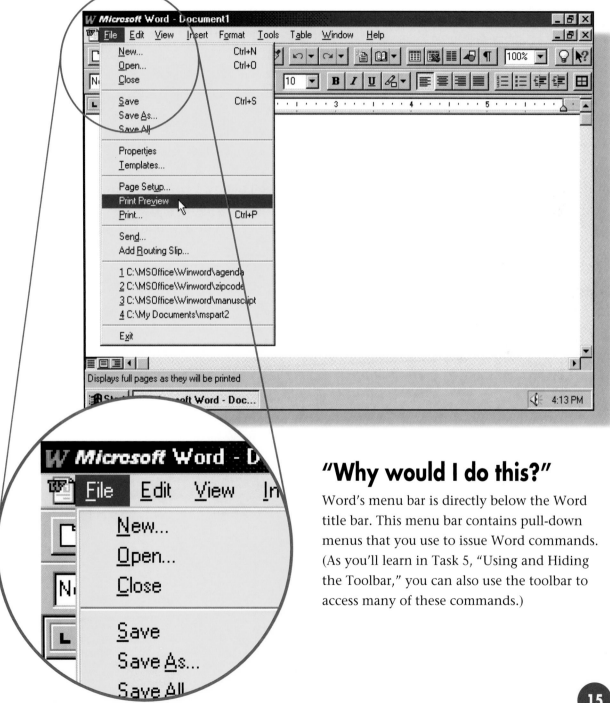

"Why would I do this?"

Word's menu bar is directly below the Word title bar. This menu bar contains pull-down menus that you use to issue Word commands. (As you'll learn in Task 5, "Using and Hiding the Toolbar," you can also use the toolbar to access many of these commands.)

1 Point to **File** in the menu bar and click the left mouse button. This opens the menu. In this case, you're opening the File menu. You see a list of file-related commands.

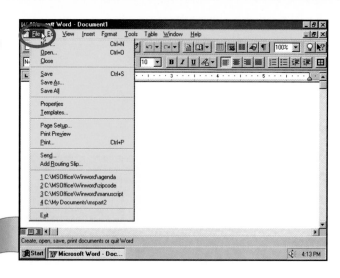

NOTE ▼

Many commands have key combinations listed beside them on the menu. These are shortcut keys you can press to issue that command, bypassing the menu system. For example, the shortcut key for the File, New command is Ctrl+N.

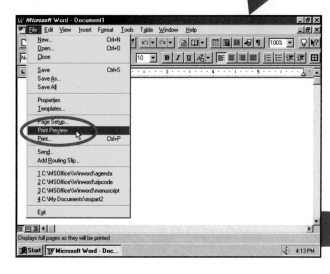

2 Point to **Print Preview** and click the left mouse button. This selects the command. In this case, you're selecting the Print Preview command, and Word displays the Print Preview window.

3 Click the **Close (X)** button on the Print Preview toolbar at the top of the screen. This closes the Print Preview window. ■

WHY WORRY?

To close a menu without making a selection, click anywhere else on the screen, outside of the menu or press Esc.

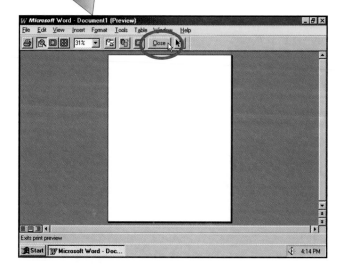

Using Shortcut Menus

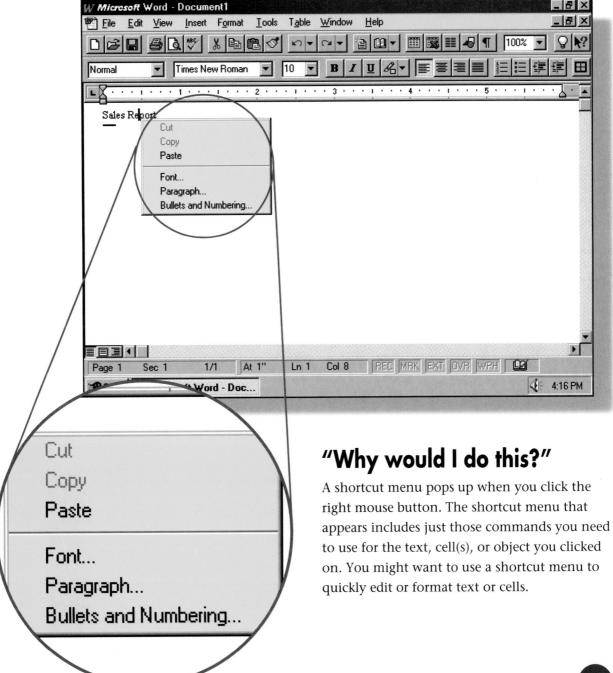

"Why would I do this?"

A shortcut menu pops up when you click the right mouse button. The shortcut menu that appears includes just those commands you need to use for the text, cell(s), or object you clicked on. You might want to use a shortcut menu to quickly edit or format text or cells.

1 Type **Sales Report**. This enters text into the document. This is the text you will change using the shortcut menu.

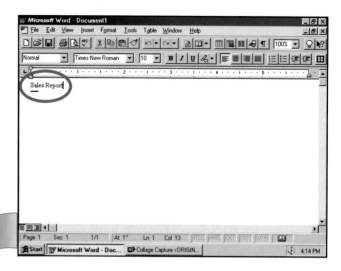

2 Point to the text and click the right mouse button to open a shortcut menu. Word displays a list of commands for editing and formatting text.

WHY WORRY?

Sometimes, you'll display a shortcut menu that doesn't have the command you want. To leave a shortcut menu without making a selection, click outside the shortcut menu or press the Esc key.

3 Click **Bullets and Numbering**. Word displays the Bullets and Numbering dialog box, and the shortcut menu disappears. Click the **Cancel** button in the dialog box to remove the dialog box. ■

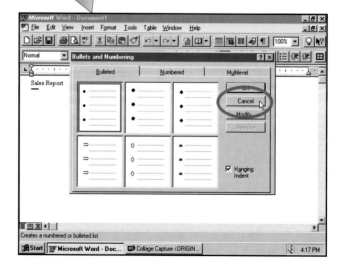

TASK 5
Using Dialog Boxes

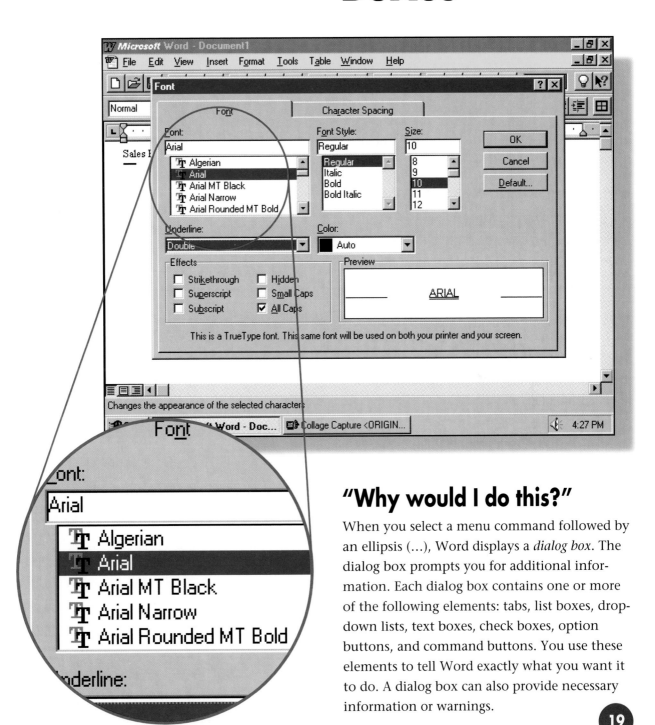

"Why would I do this?"

When you select a menu command followed by an ellipsis (...), Word displays a *dialog box*. The dialog box prompts you for additional information. Each dialog box contains one or more of the following elements: tabs, list boxes, drop-down lists, text boxes, check boxes, option buttons, and command buttons. You use these elements to tell Word exactly what you want it to do. A dialog box can also provide necessary information or warnings.

1 Open the **Format** menu and select **Font.** You see the Font dialog box.

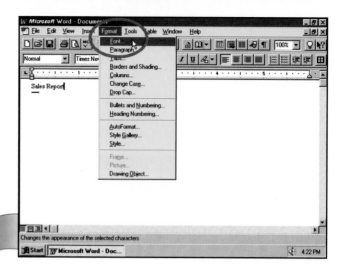

2 Click the up or down scroll arrow in the Font list box to scroll through the font list. Click a font name in the Font list box. The name of the font you select appears in the text box above the list box and in the Preview box. For example, the Arial font is selected in the figure.

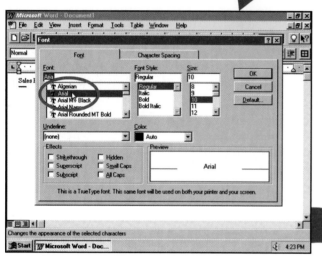

3 Click the down arrow next to the Underline box. You see a list of underline styles. Click an underline style, such as Double, and it appears in the text box at the top.

WHY WORRY?

Sometimes a drop-down list doesn't have the item you want. To leave a drop-down list without making a selection, click anywhere outside it.

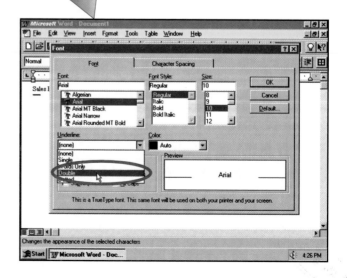

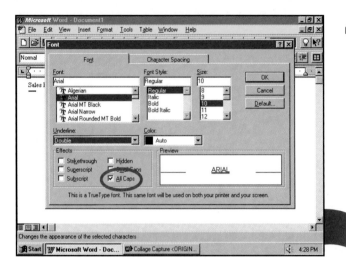

4 Click a check box to select an option in the Effects area, such as the All Caps option selected in the figure. A check mark appears in the check box, indicating that you selected the option.

NOTE ▼

Clicking again on the check box removes the check mark and tells Word to turn off that option.

5 Click a folder tab (such as the Character Spacing folder tab shown in the figure) to display another set of options. You see the options for the folder tab you selected.

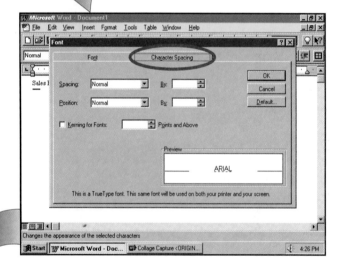

6 To accept the options you selected in the dialog box, click **OK**. To reject the options you selected, click **Cancel**. The dialog box disappears. ■

Using and Hiding the Toolbar

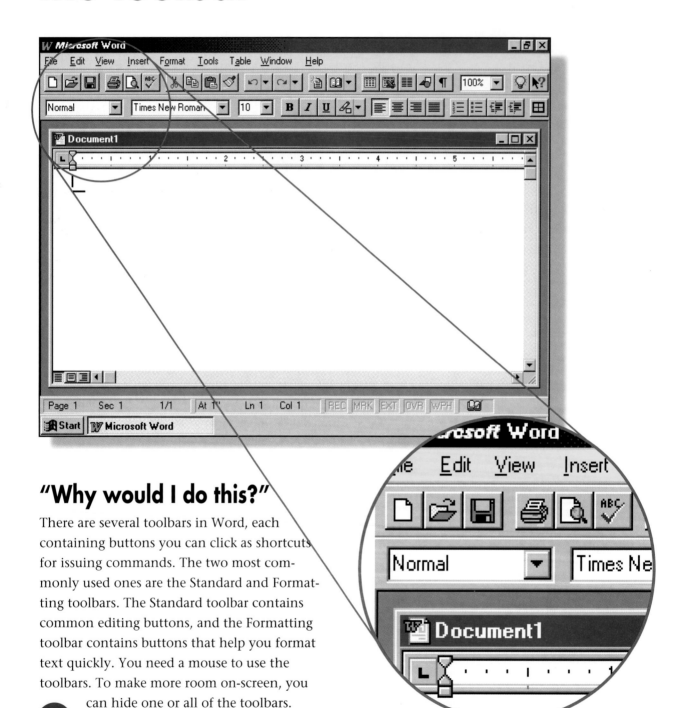

"Why would I do this?"

There are several toolbars in Word, each containing buttons you can click as shortcuts for issuing commands. The two most commonly used ones are the Standard and Formatting toolbars. The Standard toolbar contains common editing buttons, and the Formatting toolbar contains buttons that help you format text quickly. You need a mouse to use the toolbars. To make more room on-screen, you can hide one or all of the toolbars.

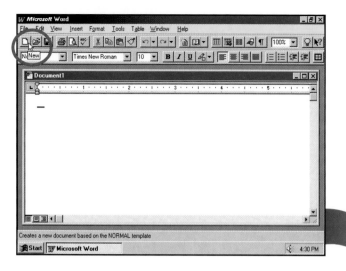

1 Point to the **New** button, the first button on the Standard toolbar, and leave the mouse pointer on the button. The button's name appears in a pale yellow box near the button. This is the ToolTip feature.

WHY WORRY?

Be sure to move the mouse pointer directly over the toolbar button. If the ToolTip does not appear, try moving the mouse pointer again and pause a few seconds.

2 Click the **New** button. Word opens a new document called DOCUMENT2 and displays it on top of DOCUMENT1.

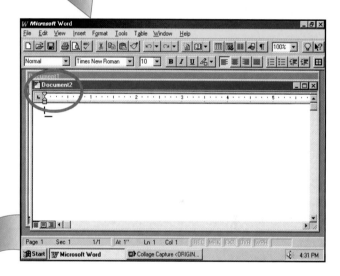

3 Click **File** in the menu bar. Then click **Close (X)**. Word closes the DOCUMENT2 document. DOCUMENT1 is now the active document again.

23

4 Open the **View** menu and select the **Toolbars** command. You see the Toolbars dialog box, which lists the available toolbars. A check mark next to the toolbar name indicates that a toolbar is displayed.

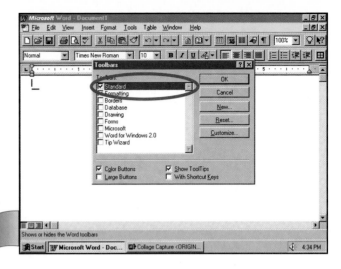

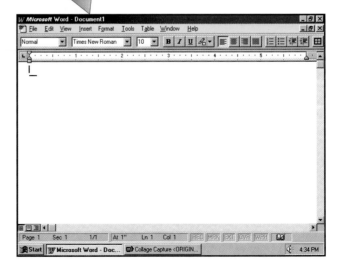

5 Click the box next to **Standard**. The check mark disappears, which tells Word not to display the Standard toolbar. Click **OK** to put the change into effect and close the dialog box.

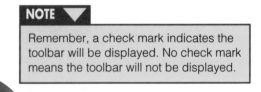

> **NOTE** ▼
>
> Remember, a check mark indicates the toolbar will be displayed. No check mark means the toolbar will not be displayed.

6 The Standard toolbar is hidden. Follow these steps again to display the toolbar. To display the toolbar, make sure there is a check mark in the check box next to the toolbar name. ■

Hiding the Ruler

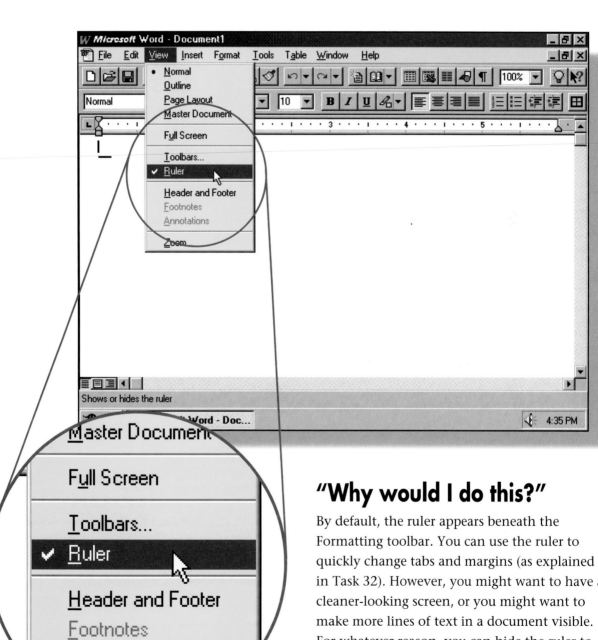

"Why would I do this?"

By default, the ruler appears beneath the Formatting toolbar. You can use the ruler to quickly change tabs and margins (as explained in Task 32). However, you might want to have a cleaner-looking screen, or you might want to make more lines of text in a document visible. For whatever reason, you can hide the ruler to make more room on-screen.

1 Open the **View** menu. You see a list of View commands. A check mark appears next to the Ruler command on the menu, which indicates that the ruler is displayed.

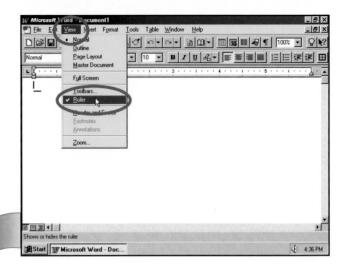

2 Click **Ruler** to remove the check mark next to it. The menu disappears, and the ruler is hidden.

> **NOTE** ▼
>
> For beginners, the screen may be less confusing with the ruler hidden.

3 If desired, select **View**, **Ruler** again to display the ruler. You will see a check mark next to Ruler on the View menu when you choose View. ■

> **NOTE** ▼
>
> The Ruler command is a toggle. If you select this command when the ruler is displayed on-screen, Word hides the ruler. If you select this command when the ruler is hidden, Word displays the ruler.

Getting Help

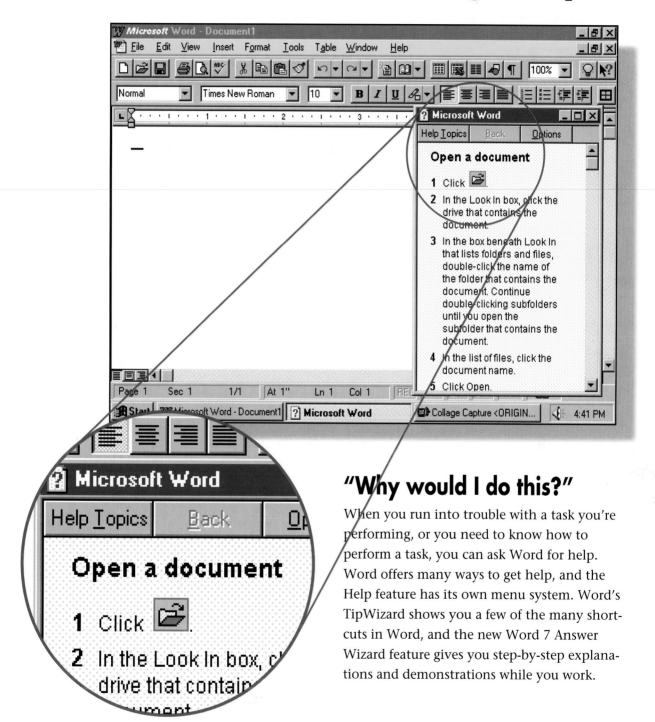

"Why would I do this?"

When you run into trouble with a task you're performing, or you need to know how to perform a task, you can ask Word for help. Word offers many ways to get help, and the Help feature has its own menu system. Word's TipWizard shows you a few of the many short-cuts in Word, and the new Word 7 Answer Wizard feature gives you step-by-step explanations and demonstrations while you work.

1 Open the **Help** menu and choose **Microsoft Word Help Topics**. Word opens the Help Topics window, and you see a list of Help topics.

> **NOTE** ▼
>
> To open Help to the specific topic you're working on, you can press F1 (Help). You can also click the What's This button (?) in the upper-right corner of a dialog box to get help on the command for which you are setting options.

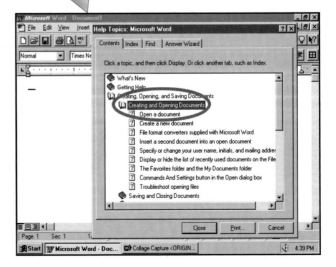

2 Each category has a book icon in front of it. Double-click the category icon for **Creating, Opening, and Saving Documents**. This selects the Help topic and displays a list of topics beneath it.

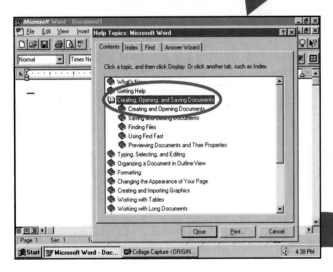

3 Double-click the category icon for **Creating and Opening Documents**. This selects the Help topic and displays a list of subtopics. In front of each topic is a topic icon, which looks like a piece of paper with a question mark.

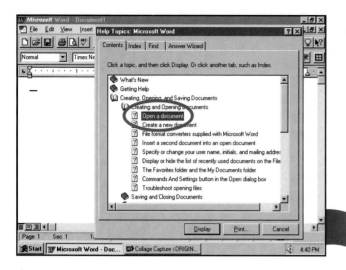

4 Double-click the topic icon for **Open a document**. Word displays the Microsoft Word Help window and closes the Help Topics dialog box. The Microsoft Word Help window contains the steps you follow to open a document.

5 Click the **Close (X)** button in the Microsoft Word Help window. Word closes the Help window.

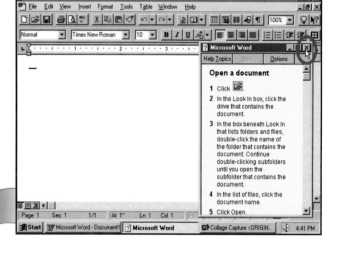

> **NOTE ▼**
>
> The TipWizard box appears when you start Word so that you can learn Word's many shortcuts. If you have memorized all the tips and don't want the TipWizard box to appear each time you start Word, just click the TipWizard button (the light bulb) on the Standard toolbar to hide the TipWizard box.

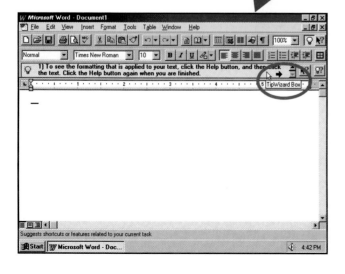

6 By default, Word displays shortcuts in the TipWizard box above the ruler. Click the up or down arrow button at the end of the TipWizard box. Clicking the down arrow button displays the next tip, and clicking the up arrow button displays the previous tip.

29

7 If a tip displays the Show Me button (a lightbulb and a ?) at the far right side of the TipWizard box, click the **Show Me** button. Word displays the Help window for the tip that appears in the TipWizard box, giving you more information.

> **NOTE** ▼
>
> If a tip suggests clicking a button on a toolbar, Word displays the button at the end of the TipWizard to the left of the Show Me button.

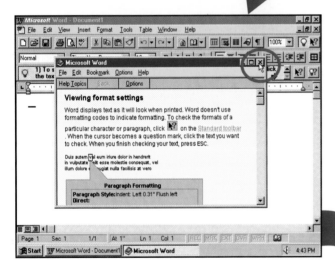

8 Click the **Close (X)** button in the Help window to close the window.

9 Click **Help** in the menu bar. Then click **Answer Wizard**. Word opens the Help Topics window. The Answer Wizard tab is selected.

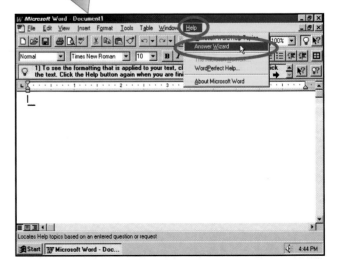

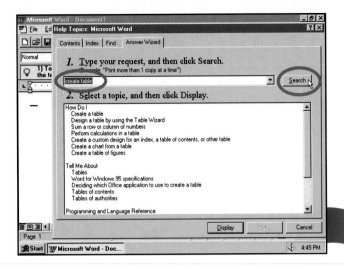

10 Type **Create table** in the text box. This enters the question you want to ask the Answer Wizard. Then click the **Search** button. You see a list of topics in the list box.

11 Double-click **Create a Table**. It opens the Microsoft Word Help window and closes the Help Topics dialog box. The Help window contains instructions on how to create a table.

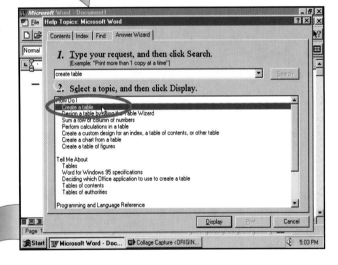

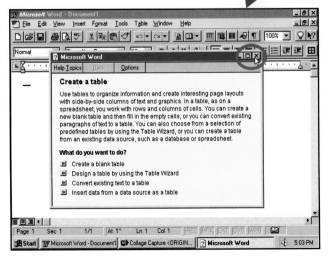

12 When you finish reading the Help information, click the **Close (X)** button to close the Help window. ■

NOTE ▼

You can return to the Help Topics dialog box by clicking the Help Topics button in the Help window instead of clicking the Close button to close the window.

PART II

Entering and Editing Data

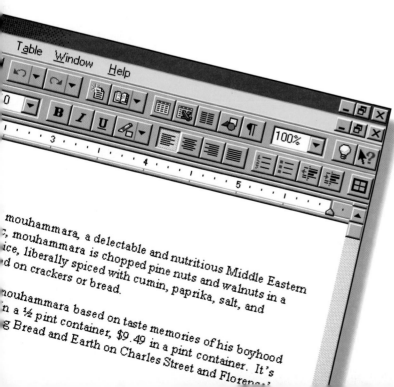

I n Part I of this book, you created a new document. You can enter text in that document, or you can create another new document.

To enter text, just start typing. As you type, text appears to the left of the insertion point, and the insertion point moves to the right. When you reach the end of a line, the insertion point automatically moves to the next line. There's no need to press Enter after each line.

When you insert or delete text, it always happens at the *insertion point*—the vertical blinking line that moves with your typed text. To insert or delete from different parts of the document, you need to learn how to move the insertion point to the desired spot. There are many ways to move around the document. You can use the arrow keys to move one character at a time. You can also use key combinations to quickly move around the document.

You can navigate around the document with the following arrow keys and key combinations:

To Move	Press
Right one character	→
Left one character	←
Up one line	↑
Down one line	↓
To the previous word	Ctrl+←
To the next word	Ctrl+→
To the beginning of a line	Home
To the end of a line	End
To the beginning of the document	Ctrl+Home
To the end of the document	Ctrl+End
To the previous screen	PgUp
To the next screen	PgDn

This part will also show you how to quickly move around the document with the mouse.

Anytime you open an existing document to continue work on it, you're adding to it. You can use some simple editing features to add text to an existing document. These features include Insert mode and Overtype mode. This part discusses both modes for adding text.

To add text to any document, you can either type in new text or cut and paste text from another document. It is even possible to merge another text file with the current one (it's called *inserting* a file).

After you enter data, you can overwrite text, insert a blank line to separate paragraphs, combine paragraphs, insert a tab, and insert page breaks. With Word for Windows' Go To command, you can jump to a specific page that is out of view.

This part also shows you how to select or highlight text. You select text to define a portion of text that you want to type over, delete, move, copy, edit, or enhance. Word for Windows highlights text you select.

You can select text with the following key combinations:

To Select	Press
One character to the right of the insertion point	Shift+→
One character to the left of the insertion point	Shift+←
One word to the right of the insertion point	Ctrl+→
One word to the left of the insertion point	Ctrl+←
One line above the insertion point	Shift+↑
One line below the insertion point	Shift+↓
From the insertion point to the end of the line	Shift+End
From the insertion point to the beginning of the line	Shift+Home

We also show you how to quickly select text with the mouse, and you learn how to delete and copy text, move text to other locations in the document, and undo mistakes. With Word's Redo command, you can reverse any Undo command you perform.

The skills that you learn in this part will save you much time and effort when entering and editing text into your documents.

Entering Text

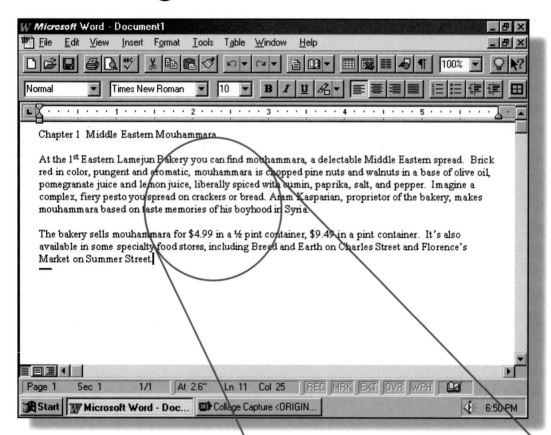

"Why would I do this?"

Typing text in Word is much faster and easier than writing on paper; it's similar to typing on a typewriter. When you reach the right margin, Word automatically "returns the carriage" for you (known as *word wrap*). The carriage return and word wrap take you to the next line. Because the paragraph becomes a single entry, editing is easier.

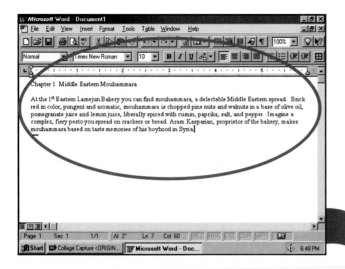

1 Type the text that appears in this figure so that your computer screen matches the screen shown here.

WHY WORRY?

If you make a mistake when typing text, use the Backspace key or Delete key to correct the entry.

2 Press **Enter**. Pressing Enter ends the paragraph. Notice that the insertion point moves to the beginning of the next line.

NOTE

Why are some words underlined with a red wavy line? Word 7's new automatic spell checking feature finds and underlines misspelled words as you type. This feature is turned on by default. To turn it off, choose Tools, Options. Click the Spelling tab and choose the Automatic Spell Checking option.

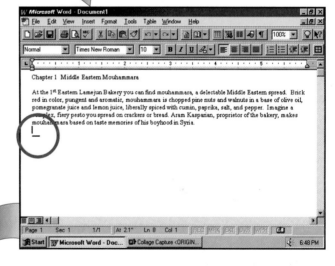

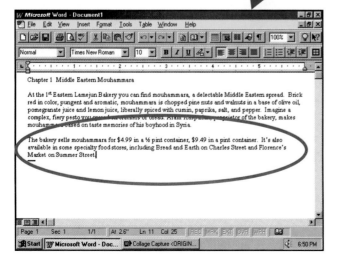

3 Press **Enter** again. Pressing Enter again inserts a blank line below the paragraph. Next, type the text that appears in this figure so your computer screen matches the screen shown here. ■

WHY WORRY?

To delete the text, click the Undo button in the Standard toolbar immediately after typing the new text.

TASK 10

Moving Around the Document

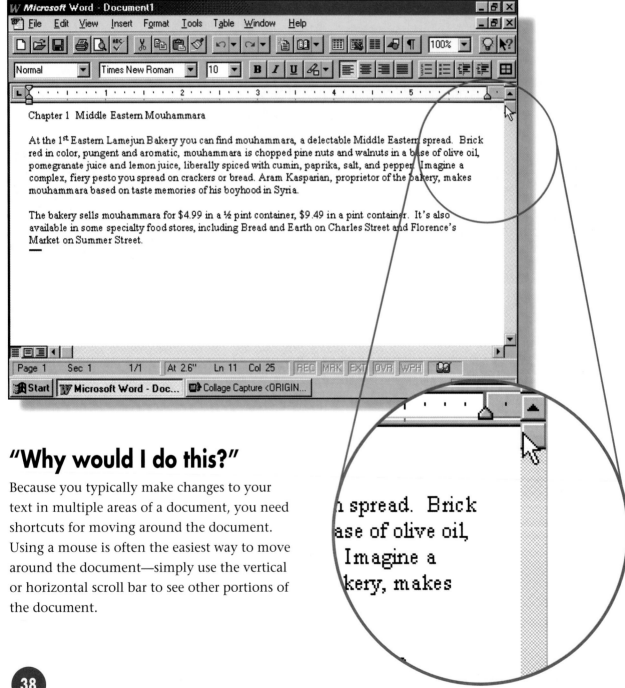

"Why would I do this?"

Because you typically make changes to your text in multiple areas of a document, you need shortcuts for moving around the document. Using a mouse is often the easiest way to move around the document—simply use the vertical or horizontal scroll bar to see other portions of the document.

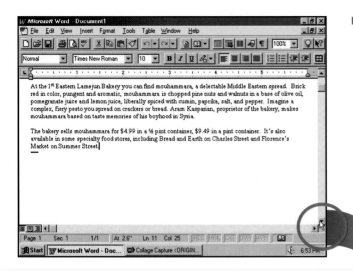

1 Click twice on the down scroll arrow at the bottom of the vertical scroll bar. Clicking the down scroll arrow moves the document down one or more lines at a time, depending on the length of the document.

NOTE ▼

You can point to the up, down, left, or right scroll bar arrow and hold down the left mouse button to scroll the document quickly in a particular direction.

2 Click twice on the up scroll arrow at the top of the vertical scroll bar. Clicking the up scroll arrow scrolls the document up one or more lines at a time, depending on the length of the document.

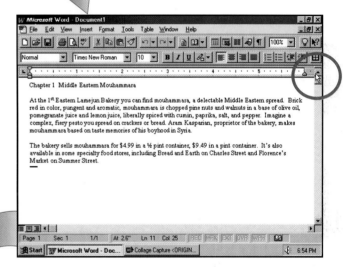

3 Click halfway down in the vertical scroll bar itself. Clicking in the scroll bar moves the document up or down one window length at a time. Here, Word displays the end of the document, and the scroll box is at the bottom of the vertical scroll bar.

4 Drag the scroll box up to the top of the vertical scroll bar. Dragging the scroll box moves the document quickly to a new location in the direction of the scroll box. In this case, Word for Windows moves to and displays the beginning of the document.

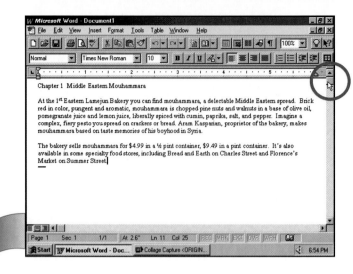

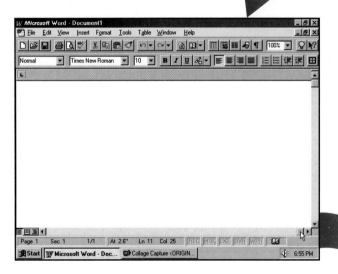

5 Drag the scroll box to the far right of the horizontal scroll bar. Dragging the scroll box moves the document quickly to a new location in the direction of the scroll box. In this case, Word for Windows moves the document to the left and displays the right side of the document.

WHY WORRY?

If you run out of room to move the mouse on your desktop or mouse pad, just lift the mouse and move it to a new location. The mouse pointer will not move when the mouse is in the air.

6 Drag the scroll box to the far left of the horizontal scroll bar. Dragging the scroll box moves the document quickly to a new location in the direction of the scroll box. In this case, Word for Windows moves the document to the right and displays the left side of the document. ■

NOTE ▼

Keep in mind that any action you perform on a vertical scroll bar you can also perform on the horizontal scroll bar.

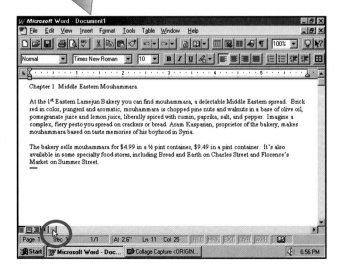

Adding and Overwriting Text

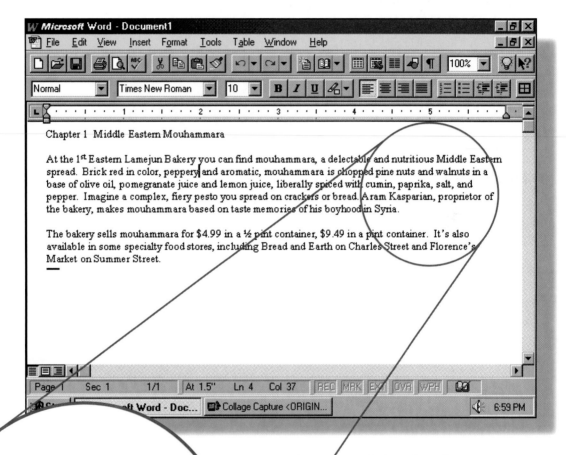

"Why would I do this?"

By default, Word is in Insert mode. In Insert mode, you type text at the insertion point, and the existing text moves forward to make room for the new text. Overwriting text means replacing the existing text with new text. This is handy when you want to correct typing errors.

1 Click before the word *Middle* to place the insertion point where you want to insert text. You can place the insertion point by clicking the location or by using the arrow keys.

NOTE ▼

The Insert key is a toggle. Do not press the Insert key to insert text. Pressing the Insert key puts Word for Windows in Overtype mode.

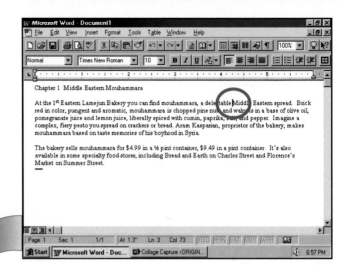

2 Type **and nutritious**. Then press the **Spacebar**. Word inserts the new text and pushes the existing text to the right, adding a space between the new text and the original text.

WHY WORRY?

To delete the text, click the Undo button in the Standard toolbar immediately after typing the new text. Or, simply delete the text.

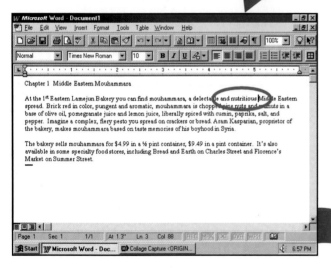

3 Click before the *p* in *pungent* to place the insertion point where you want to over-write text. You can place the insertion point by clicking the location or by using the arrow keys.

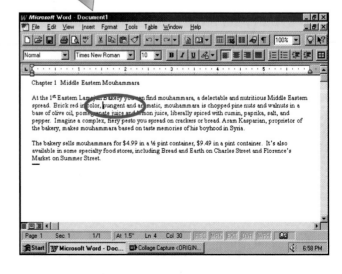

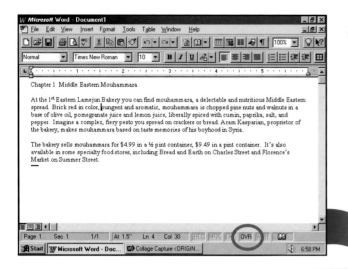

4 Press **Insert** to put Word for Windows in Overtype mode. The indicator OVR appears in the status bar at the bottom of the screen. Text you type now will overwrite existing text.

NOTE ▼

The Insert key is a toggle. You press this key one time to turn on Overtype mode. You press it again to turn off Overtype mode and return to Insert mode.

5 Type **peppery**. Word for Windows deletes the original text and replaces it with *peppery*.

NOTE ▼

You can also select the text you want to replace and start typing. The new text replaces all the selected text.

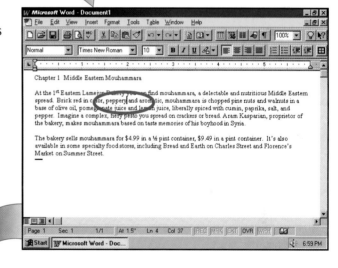

6 Press **Insert**. The indicator OVR disappears from the status bar. Overtype mode is turned off. ■

WHY WORRY?

To change one letter at a time, click the Undo button on the Standard toolbar immediately after overwriting the text.

43

TASK 12

Separating and Combining Paragraphs

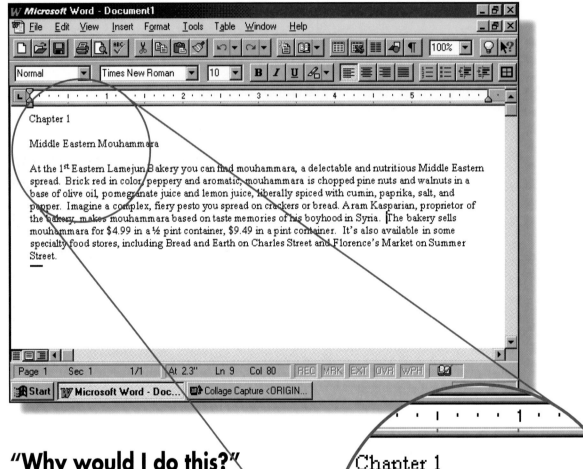

"Why would I do this?"

Unlike when you type on a typewriter, you don't have to press Enter at the end of each line. When text reaches the end of the line, Word automatically wraps the text to the next line. Press Enter to insert a hard return at the end of a short line, to place a blank line between paragraphs, or to end a paragraph.

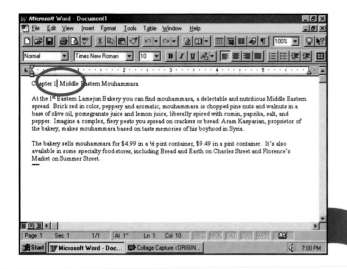

1 Press **Ctrl+Home** to move to the top of the document, and then click after *Chapter 1*. Thisplaces the insertion point where you want to insert a blank line.

2 Press **Enter**. Pressing Enter ends the current paragraph; Word inserts a paragraph mark in the document.

NOTE ▼

By default, actual paragraph marks (¶) do not appear on-screen. If you want to display paragraph marks, click the Show/Hide Paragraph button (¶) on the Standard toolbar.

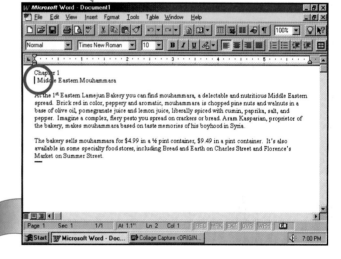

3 Press **Enter**. The first two lines of text are now separated by a blank line. (You can press **Delete** twice to delete the two spaces.)

4 Click after *Syria.* at the end of the first paragraph. This places the insertion point at the end of the first paragraph. Be sure to click after the period.

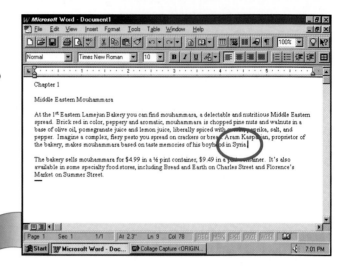

5 Press **Delete**. Pressing the Delete key deletes the paragraph mark at the end of the current paragraph.

◀ WHY WORRY?

To split the paragraphs and add a blank line between them, place the insertion point where you want the break to appear. Then press Enter two times.

6 Press **Delete** again. Then press the **Spacebar** twice. Pressing the Delete key again deletes the blank line between the paragraphs. The second paragraph moves up next to the first paragraph. Pressing the Spacebar inserts two spaces between the two sentences. ∎

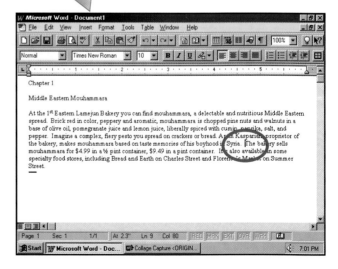

Selecting Text

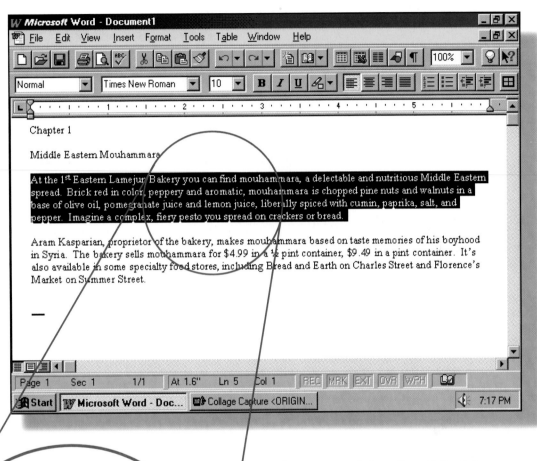

"Why would I do this?"

Knowing how to select text is essential
because most of the commands and options in
Word for Windows operate on the selected text.
For example, you might want to select a title so
you can issue the command to make it bold or
larger. You can select any amount of text with
the mouse: a block of text, a word, a line, a
sentence, or a paragraph.

1 Place the mouse pointer at the beginning of the text you want to select, hold down the left mouse button, and drag the mouse pointer across the text you want to select. This selects the amount of text you specify.

WHY WORRY?

If you selected the wrong text, simply click on any text in the document. Then start over.

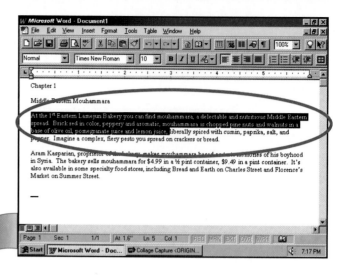

2 Double-click anywhere in the word *delectable* to select only that word.

WHY WORRY?

If you double-click a word to select and drag it, and then click (and hold) for the drag operation too quickly, the entire paragraph will be unintentionally selected. To avoid this, pause briefly before you click-and-hold to drag a word.

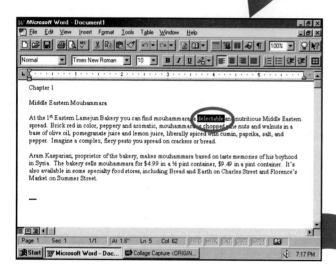

3 Click in the left margin next to the line of text to select a line of text.

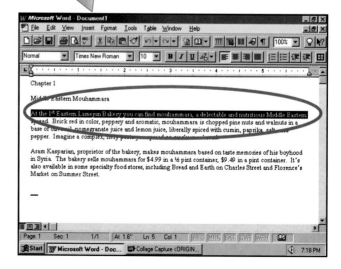

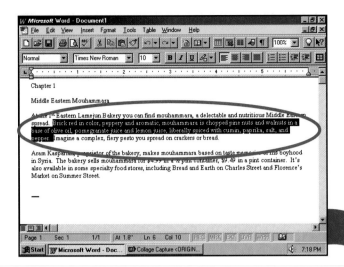

4 Hold down **Ctrl** and click anywhere within a sentence. This selects the sentence.

5 Double-click in the left margin next to the paragraph to select a whole paragraph.

> **NOTE** ▼
>
> You can also triple-click anywhere inside the paragraph to select a paragraph.

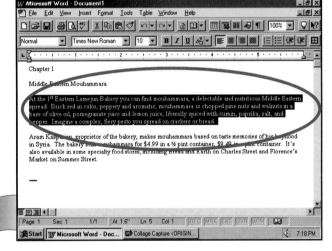

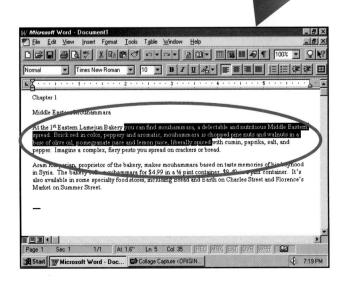

6 Position the mouse pointer at the beginning of the text you want to select, click the left mouse button, and then hold down **Shift** as you click at the end of the block of text. ∎

Deleting Text and Using Undo

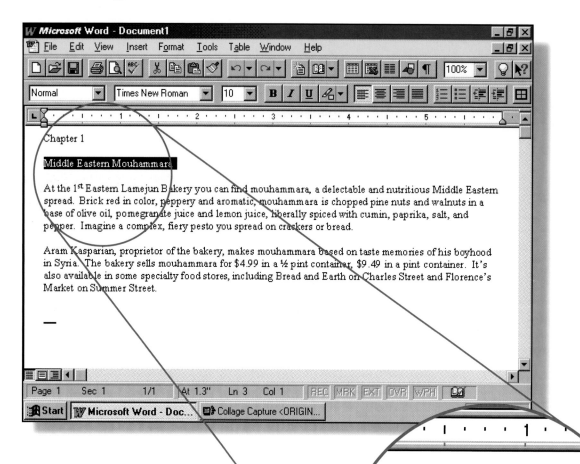

"Why would I do this?"

Sometimes you may find that text you initially typed into the document is incorrect and needs to be changed. Instead of overwriting the text to remove the entry, you can select any amount of text and then press the Delete key. To delete just one character, use the Delete or Backspace key. If you accidentally delete the wrong text, you can use the Undo feature to restore it.

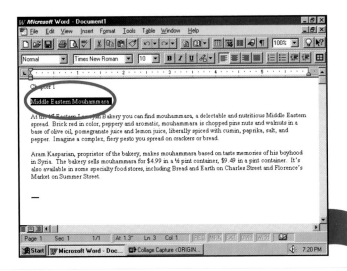

1 Click in the left margin next to the chapter title. This selects the paragraph *Middle Eastern Mouhammara,* the text you want to delete.

2 Press **Delete**. Word for Windows deletes the text. The remaining text moves up (or over) to fill in the gap.

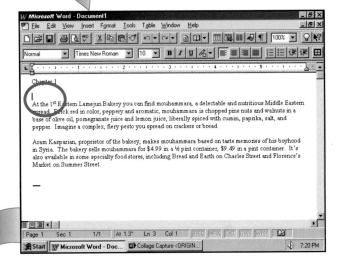

3 Click the **Undo** button on the Standard toolbar. Word for Windows restores the deleted text. As you can see, the document returns to its original form. Click outside the selected text to deselect the text. ■

WHY WORRY?

Click the Redo button (the button that contains an arrow that curves to the right and down) on the Standard toolbar to "undo" the Undo.

TASK 15
Copying Text

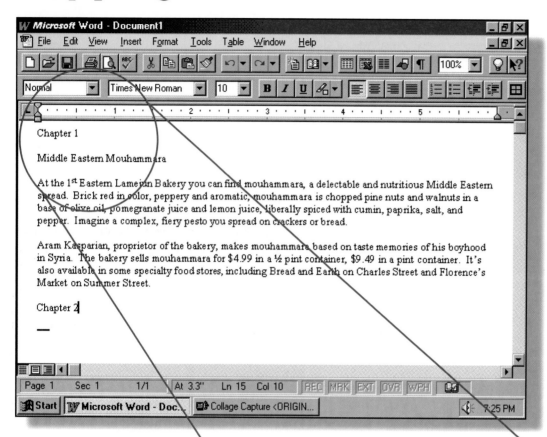

"Why would I do this?"

You can save the time of retyping information in the document by copying text over and over again. For example, you might want to copy a paragraph from one page to another page. That way, you wouldn't have to type the paragraph over again, which saves you time and keystrokes.

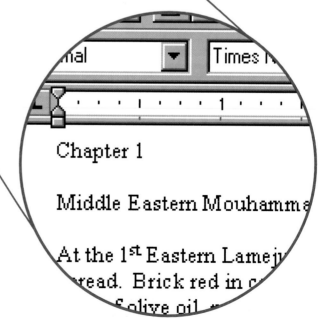

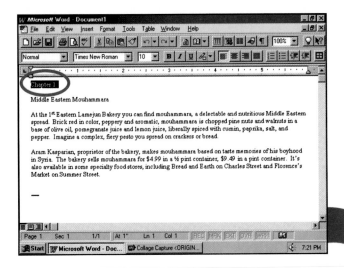

1 Click in the left margin next to the chapter name. This selects the paragraph you want to copy—in this case, *Chapter 1*.

2 Click the **Copy** button (the button that contains two pieces of paper) on the Standard toolbar. Clicking the Copy button copies the text to the Clipboard. The Clipboard is a temporary holding area for text and graphics.

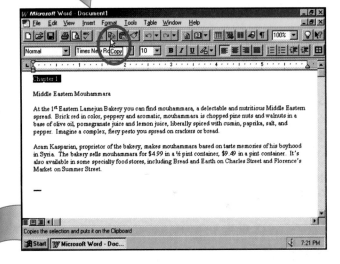

3 Click at the end of the document, below the second paragraph to place the insertion point where you want the copied text to appear.

4 Click the **Paste** button (the button that contains a piece of paper on top of a clipboard) on the Standard toolbar. The copied text now appears in the new location (as well as the original location).

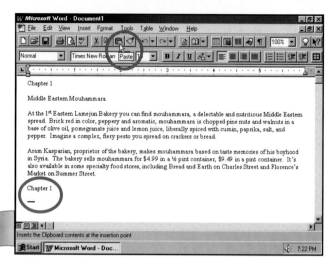

5 Click before the *1* in *Chapter 1*.
Press **Insert** to turn on Overtype mode.

NOTE ▼

To copy text using drag-and-drop, select the text. Click and hold down the Ctrl key and the mouse button. You see a plus sign above and a small box under the mouse pointer. Drag the text to the new location. Release the Ctrl key and the mouse button. You can also use the Ctrl+C and Ctrl+V key combinations to select the Copy and Paste commands.

6 Type **2** and press **Insert** again. This changes the chapter number and switches you back to Insert mode. ■

WHY WORRY?

If you copied the wrong text or copied the data to the wrong location, click the Undo button on the Standard toolbar to undo the most recent copy, or delete the copied text. Then start over.

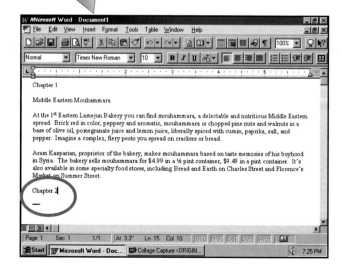

Moving Text

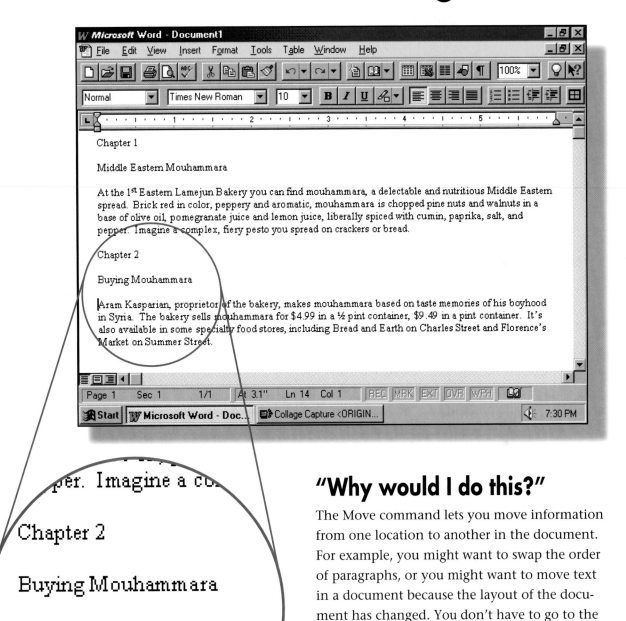

"Why would I do this?"

The Move command lets you move information from one location to another in the document. For example, you might want to swap the order of paragraphs, or you might want to move text in a document because the layout of the document has changed. You don't have to go to the new location, enter the same text, and then erase the text in the old location.

1 Click in the left margin next to *Chapter 2*. This step selects the paragraph you want to move.

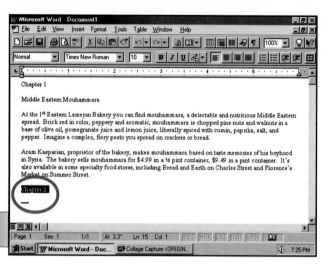

2 Click the **Cut** button (the button that shows scissors) on the Standard toolbar. Clicking the Cut button cuts the text from the document and places it on the Clipboard (a temporary holding area). The text no longer appears in its original location.

3 Click before the *A* in *Aram* at the beginning of the second paragraph. This places the insertion point where you want to move the text.

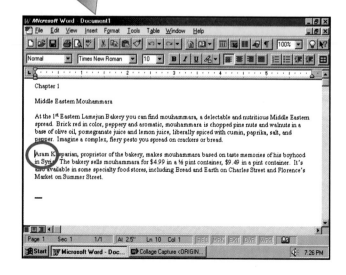

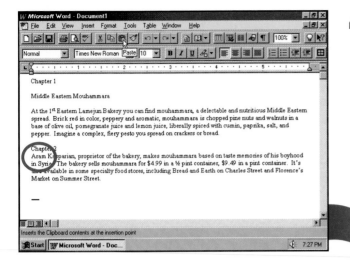

4 Click the **Paste** button (the button that contains a piece of paper on top of a clipboard) on the Standard toolbar to paste the text in the new location. The text now appears in the new location.

NOTE ▼

To use drag-and-drop to move the text, select the text. Click and hold down the mouse button. You see a small box under the mouse pointer. Drag the text to the new location. Release the mouse button.

5 Press **Enter** to insert a hard return and add a blank line.

NOTE ▼

You can also use the Ctrl+X and Ctrl+V key combinations to select the Cut and Paste commands respectively.

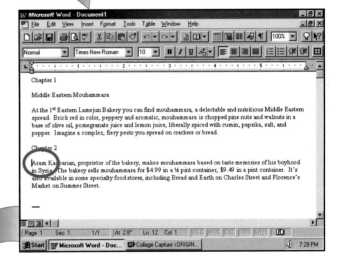

6 Type **Buying Mouhammara** and press **Enter** twice. This adds a chapter title and inserts a hard return and a blank line. ■

WHY WORRY?

If you moved the wrong text or moved the text to the wrong location, click the Undo button on the Standard toolbar to undo the most recent move. Then start over.

57

TASK 17

Inserting a Tab

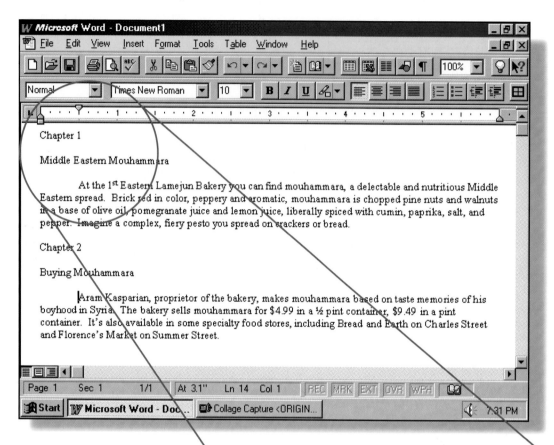

"Why would I do this?"

As you do when typing on a typewriter, you press the Tab key to insert a tab. You might want to insert a tab at the beginning of a paragraph to indent the text from the left margin. Or, you might want to use tabs in a memo heading to insert space between the headings and the memo information.

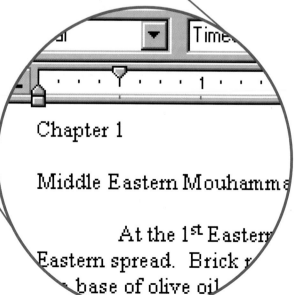

58

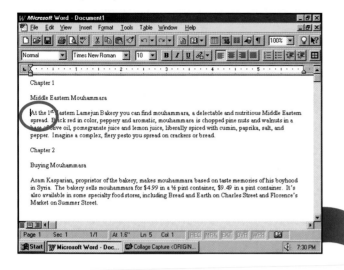

1 Click before *At* in the first sentence. The insertion point is where you want to insert a tab (at the beginning of the paragraph).

NOTE ▼

By default, tab marks (→) do not appear on-screen. If you want to display tab marks, click the Show/Hide Paragraph button on the Standard toolbar. Even with the display turned on, you will not see tab marks at the beginning of paragraphs—only on blank lines and within paragraphs.

2 Press **Tab** on the keyboard. Pressing Tab inserts a tab and moves the insertion point to the next tab stop. As you can see, the first sentence begins at the tab stop. Word for Windows provides a default tab stop every 1/2 inch. However, you can change the tab settings.

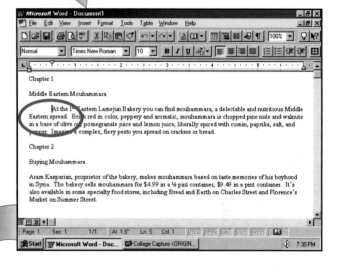

3 Click before *Aram* at the beginning of the second paragraph. Press **Tab** to insert a tab. As you can see, the first sentence in the paragraph begins at the tab stop. ■

WHY WORRY?

To delete the tab, press the Backspace key.

59

TASK 18
Inserting a Page Break

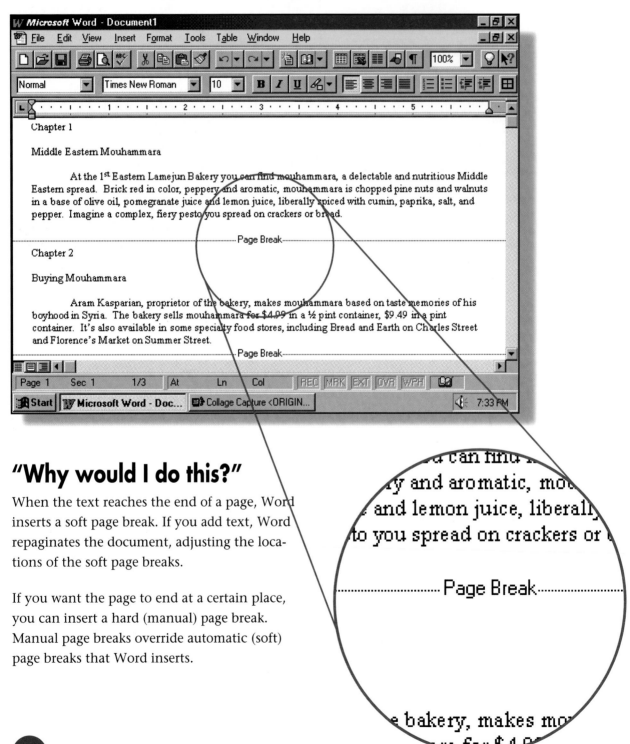

"Why would I do this?"

When the text reaches the end of a page, Word inserts a soft page break. If you add text, Word repaginates the document, adjusting the locations of the soft page breaks.

If you want the page to end at a certain place, you can insert a hard (manual) page break. Manual page breaks override automatic (soft) page breaks that Word inserts.

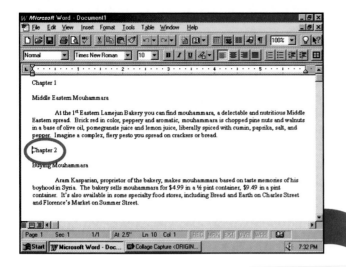

1 Click before the *C* in *Chapter 2*. This places the insertion point where you want the new page to begin. Remember that you can place the insertion point by using the mouse or the arrow keys.

NOTE ▼

A page break appears as a dotted line on-screen. The dots are farther apart on a soft page break than they are on a hard page break.

2 Press **Ctrl+Enter** to insert a hard page break. A dotted line appears with the words Page Break in the middle. When you print the document, a new page will begin where you inserted the page break.

WHY WORRY?

To remove the page break, click the Undo button on the Standard toolbar immediately after inserting the page break. Or, click on the page break to select it and press Delete.

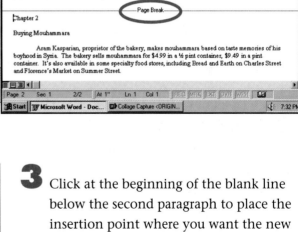

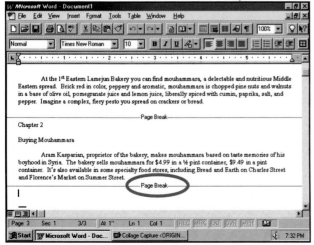

3 Click at the beginning of the blank line below the second paragraph to place the insertion point where you want the new page to begin. Then press **Ctrl+Enter** to insert a hard page break. The document now contains three pages. ■

Going to a Specific Page

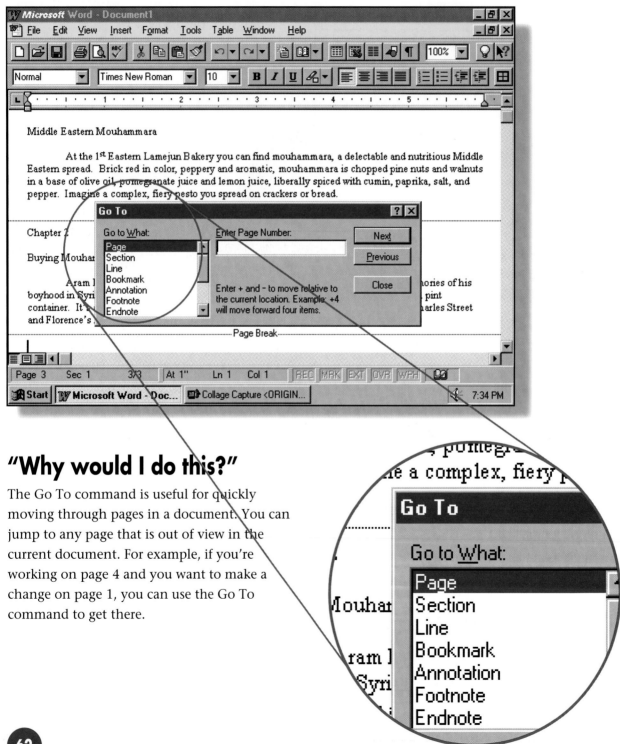

"Why would I do this?"

The Go To command is useful for quickly moving through pages in a document. You can jump to any page that is out of view in the current document. For example, if you're working on page 4 and you want to make a change on page 1, you can use the Go To command to get there.

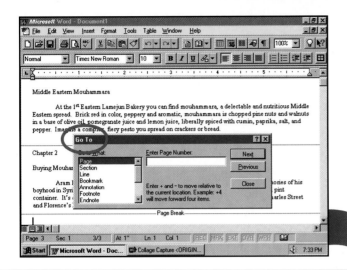

1 Click on **Edit** and select the **Go To** command. Word for Windows opens the Go To dialog box. The insertion point is in the Enter Page Number text box.

2 Type **1**. Typing 1 tells Word for Windows you want to go to page 1.

WHY WORRY?

If you mistakenly move to the wrong page, repeat the Go To command, but type the correct page number to move to the page you want.

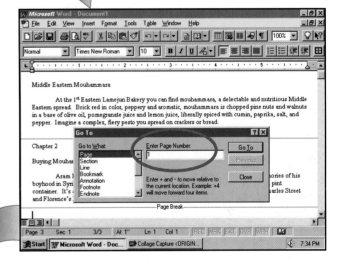

3 Click **Go To**, and page 1 becomes the current page. The page indicator on the far left side of the status bar shows Page 1, and the insertion point moves to the top of page 1. Click the **Close** button to close the Go To dialog box. ■

PART III
Managing Files

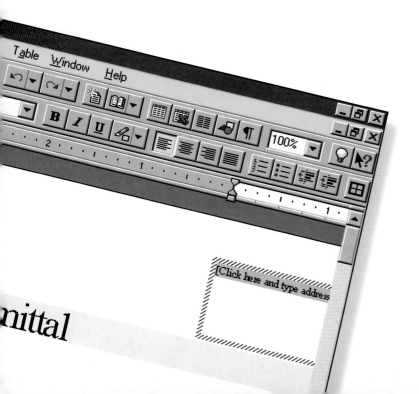

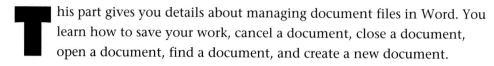

This part gives you details about managing document files in Word. You learn how to save your work, cancel a document, close a document, open a document, find a document, and create a new document.

It is a good idea to save your file every 5 or 10 minutes. If you don't save your work, you could lose it. Suppose you've been working on a worksheet for a few hours and your power goes off unexpectedly—an air-conditioning repair man at your office shorts out the power, a thunderstorm hits, or something else causes a power loss. If you haven't saved, you lose all your hard work. You should also make backup copies of your files on floppy disks from time to time.

By default, Word automatically saves your work to a backup file every 10 minutes. The backup file's name consists of the same name as your original document except that the backup file type is BAK (for example, LETTER.BAK). This serves as a safety net to prevent you from accidentally losing your work. If your power goes off, when you turn on your computer again, Word opens the backup file automatically.

Saving a file that you previously saved is slightly different from saving a newly created document. When you save a document you've saved before, you save the current version on-screen and overwrite the original version on disk. This means you always have the most current version of your file stored on disk. If you want to keep both versions—the on-screen version and the original— you can use the File Save As command to save the on-screen version with a different name. Saving a file with a new name gives you two copies of the same document with differences in their data. When you save a file with a new name, you can also save the file in a different folder or drive.

Saving a document does not remove it from the screen. You have to close the document. Whether you've saved a document or not, you can close it using the File Close command.

The File Open command lets you preview a document before opening it. That way, you can see if it is the document you want to open. A list of the most recently used files appears at the bottom of the File menu. You can choose a file from this list to open a document quickly.

Word's Search for Files feature lets you search for a document quickly using any search criteria. For example, you can find a document on a disk by using its file name or folder as search criteria. You choose the Open command and enter the search criteria in the Open dialog box. The search criteria can include text and the last modified time period. Word quickly finds the file you want to use.

In this part, you also learn how to create a document using a template and a wizard. A template provides a pattern for shaping a document. When you create a new document, you can use a template that contains boilerplate text, styles, glossary items, macros, a menu, key, and toolbar assignments. A wizard is a special template that guides you through the creation of a document. A wizard template displays dialog boxes, messages, and graphics that tell you how to fill in a template or create forms.

Also in this part, you are introduced to the essential file management skills that you will need in order to work with any files in Word.

TASK 20

Saving a Document

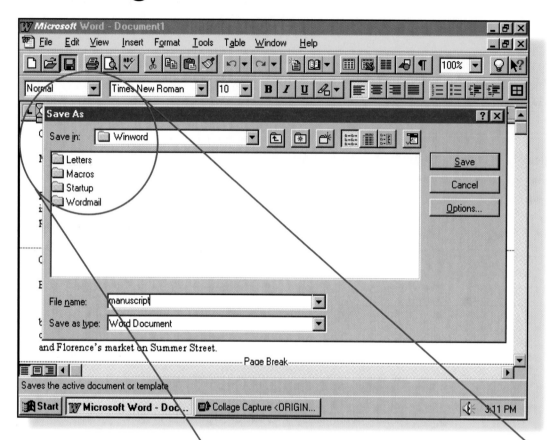

"Why would I do this?"

Until you save the document, your data is not stored on disk. You can lose your data if something, such as a power loss, happens. When you need the document again, you can retrieve it from the disk. Save your work every few minutes and at the end of a work session. Then close the document if you want to clear the screen. Word also lets you close a previously saved document without saving the changes.

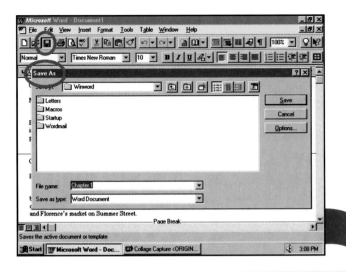

1 Click the **Save** button on the Standard toolbar. The first time you save the document, Word displays the Save As dialog box. The Save As dialog box lists current folders and the current drive.

NOTE ▼

To save your documents in a different folder, click on the Up One Level button on the Save toolbar, and then double-click on the folder you want in the Save In box. Now you can save your documents in this folder.

2 Type **MANUSCRIPT** in the File name text box as the file name you want to assign to the document. You can type as many characters as you want using upper- or lowercase. Do not use spaces or punctuation.

NOTE ▼

To save the document with a different name, choose File Save As. Type a new name in the File Name text box. Choose a different file type, drive, and folder, if necessary. Then choose OK.

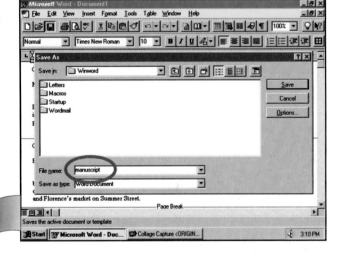

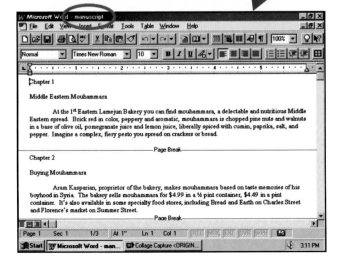

3 Click **Save**. This step accepts the file name and returns you to the document. The file name, MANUSCRIPT, appears in the title bar. ■

WHY WORRY?

If you type a file name that already exists, Word displays an alert box that asks `Replace existing file?` Click Cancel to return to the Save As dialog box, and then type a new name.

Closing a Document

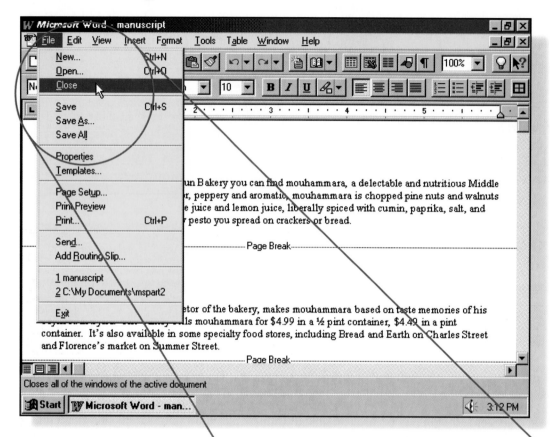

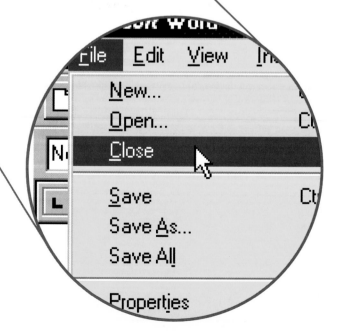

"Why would I do this?"

When you no longer want to work with a document, you can use the File Close command to close the document. Then you can use the Open button on the Standard toolbar to reopen a closed document, you can use the New button on the Standard toolbar to create a new document, or you can exit Word. You can open more than one document at once; you don't have to close a document before opening another.

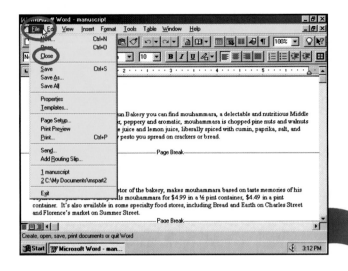

1 Click **File** in the menu bar to open the File menu. Click on **Close**.

2 If you have not made changes, Word closes the document. Now you see just two menu options: File and Help. From here, you can open a document or create a new document.

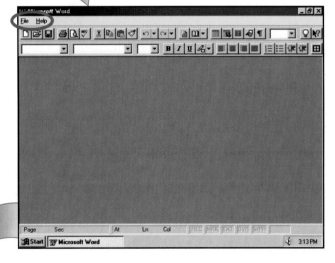

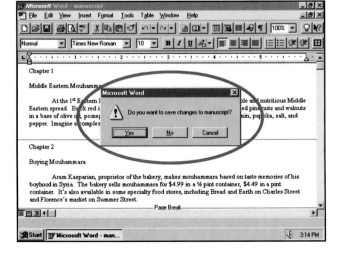

3 If you have made changes, Word displays an alert box that reminds you to save the changes. Choose **Yes** to save the changes and close the document. If you don't want to save the changes, choose No to ignore them and close the document. ■

Opening a Document

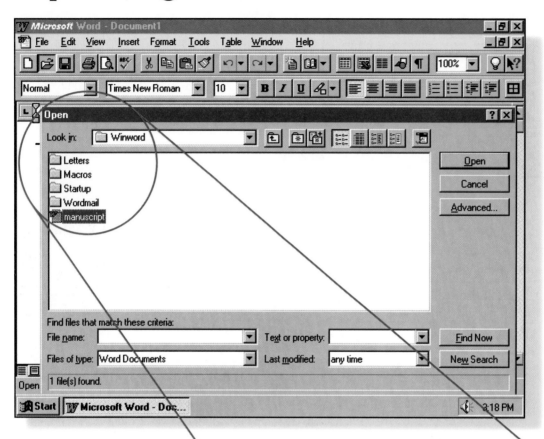

"Why would I do this?"

After you save a document, you can view it again or make changes to it later. The number of documents you can open at one time will depend on your system memory.

If you want to work with a file again, use the Open button on the Standard toolbar to preview and open the closed document file.

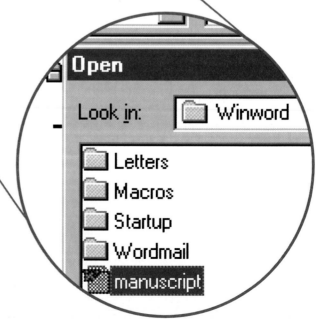

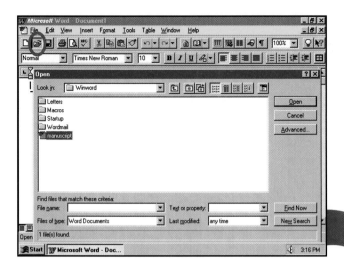

1 Click the **Open** button on the Standard toolbar. You see the Open dialog box. The insertion point is in the File name text box.

2 If necessary, click the drop-down arrow at the end of the Look in box and click the folder in the files and folders list. To move up a folder level, click the Up One Level button on the Open toolbar. If you double-click a subfolder, its contents appear in the files and folders list.

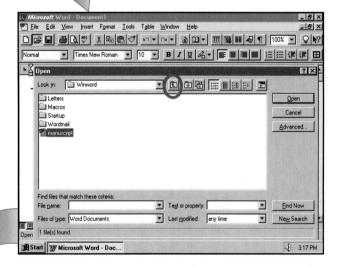

3 Click on the **MANUSCRIPT** file to select the file.

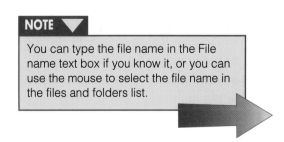

NOTE

You can type the file name in the File name text box if you know it, or you can use the mouse to select the file name in the files and folders list.

73

4 Click the **Preview** button on the Open toolbar. Word displays the document in the Preview window on the right side of the Open dialog box.

NOTE ▼

You can use the scroll bar in the Preview window to scroll through the document.

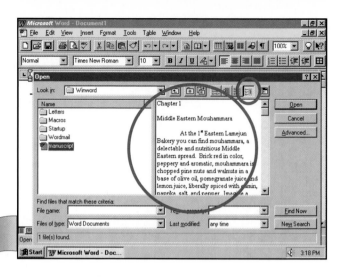

5 Click the **List** button. Word displays the list of file names on the left side of the Open dialog box. Select the file and click the **Open** button.

NOTE ▼

The most recently used files appear at the bottom of the File menu. To open a file quickly, click File and then click the file you want to open.

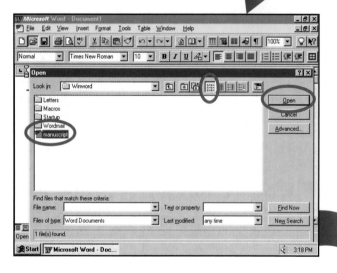

6 Word displays the document on-screen. The file name appears in the title bar. ■

WHY WORRY?

If you open the wrong document, close the document and try again.

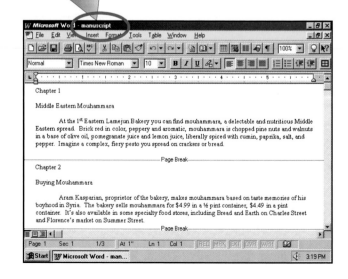

Finding a Document

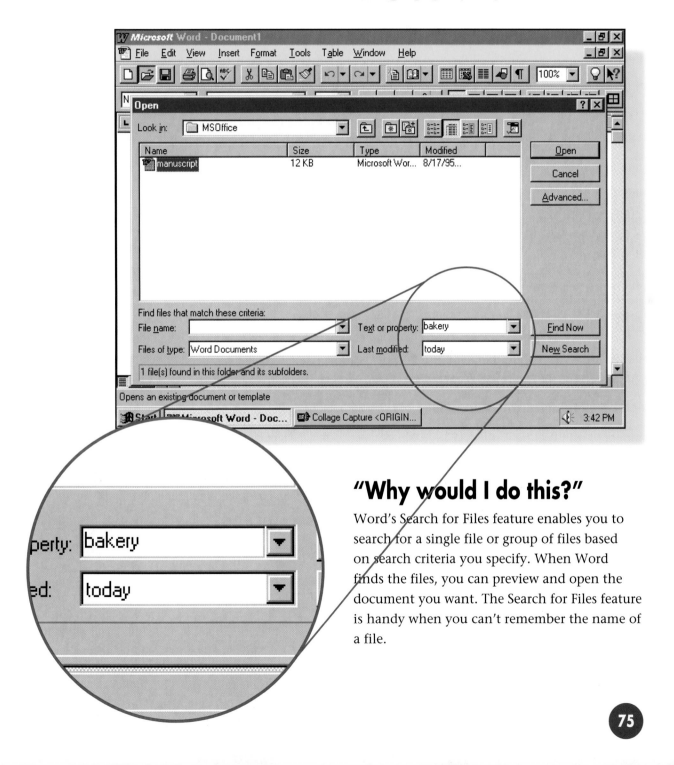

"Why would I do this?"

Word's Search for Files feature enables you to search for a single file or group of files based on search criteria you specify. When Word finds the files, you can preview and open the document you want. The Search for Files feature is handy when you can't remember the name of a file.

1 Click the **Open** button on the Standard toolbar. Word displays the Open dialog box.

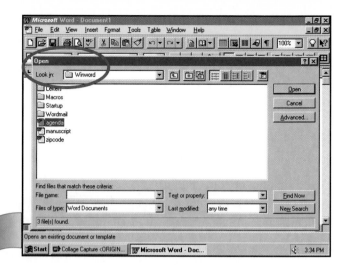

2 Type text in the Text or property text box at the bottom of the Open dialog box. For example, type **bakery** to find any document that contains the word *bakery*.

3 Click the Last Modified drop-down arrow. The Last Modified list appears. Choose **Today** to find documents you've worked with today.

NOTE ▼

Choose a date from the Last Modified drop-down list box, and then click Find Now. Word lists the files found based on the search criteria. Click New Search to clear the search criteria.

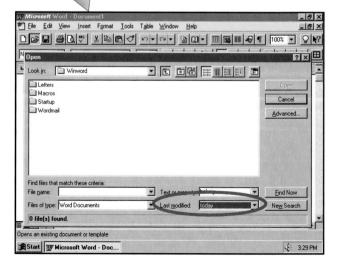

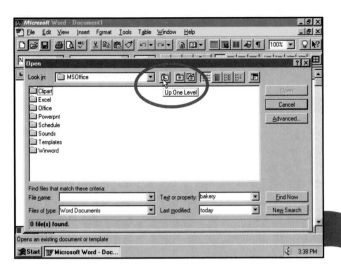

4 Click the Up One Level button on the Open toolbar and select the drive you want to search.

NOTE ▼

To search all subfolders, click the Commands and Settings button on the Open toolbar. Then choose Search Subfolders from the menu.

5 Click the **Find Now** button in the Open dialog box. Word displays a list of the files that match your search criteria. Select the one you want.

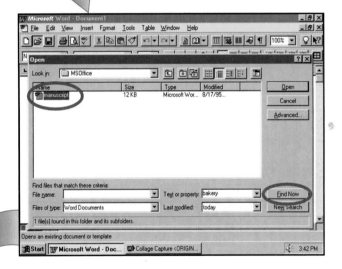

6 Click the **New Search** button to clear the current search criteria and restore the list to all files and folders for Drive C. To close the Open dialog box, click the **Cancel** button. ■

WHY WORRY?

When Word doesn't find any files based on the specified search criteria, just click the New Search button and try again.

TASK 24

Creating a New Document

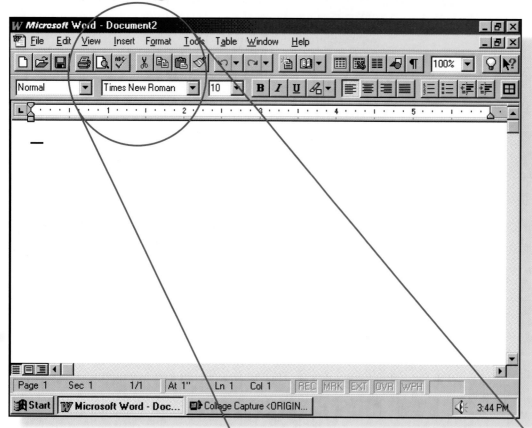

"Why would I do this?"

Word presents a new, blank document each time you start the program. You can create another new document at any time, such as when you have saved and closed the active document and want to begin a new one.

78

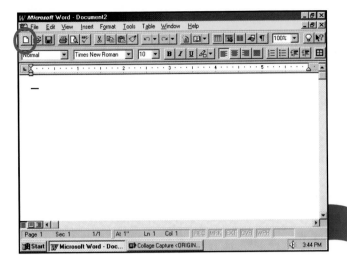

1 Click the **New** button on the Standard toolbar. A blank document appears on-screen. This document is titled DOCUMENT2 (the number varies depending on the number of documents you have created during this session).

NOTE ▼

When you start Word, the program automatically displays a blank document. You don't have to use the File New command in this case.

2 Click **File** in the menu bar. You see a list of file-related commands. Click **Close**. Word closes the document. ■

NOTE ▼

If you have more than one document open, you can switch among documents by choosing Window on the menu bar. Then choose a document from the list at the bottom of the Window menu.

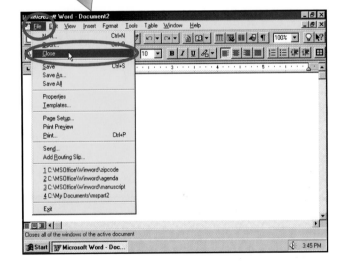

Using a Template

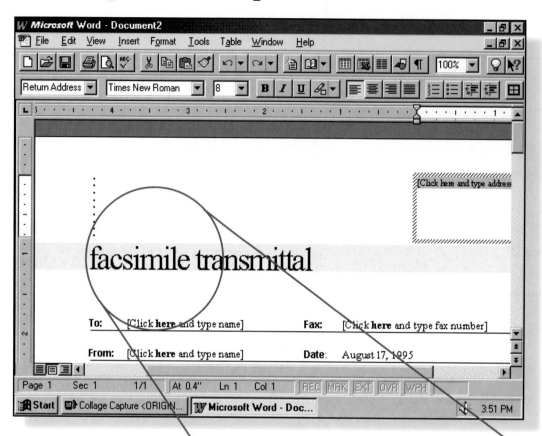

"Why would I do this?"

By default, when you create a new document, Word uses the NORMAL.DOT template, which contains the standard document settings. However, you can choose to create documents with multiple other templates. Word provides several families of templates that are organized in categories: General, Publications, Other Documents, Letters & Faxes, Memos, and Reports. You can use a template at any time to standardize types of documents that you frequently use.

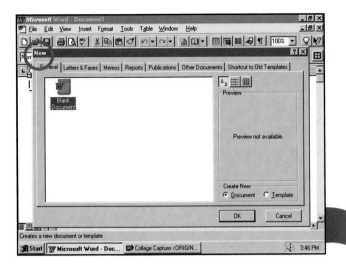

Click **File** in the menu bar. Then click **New**. You see the New dialog box.

NOTE

When you create a new document based on a template, you must use the File, New command, not the New button on the Standard toolbar. The New button doesn't display the New dialog box.

Click the **Letters & Faxes** folder tab. You see icons that represent various letters and faxes.

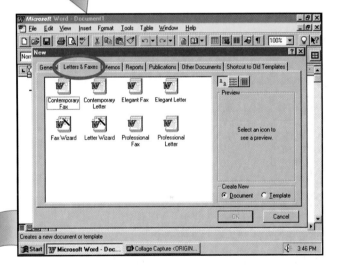

Select the template icon you want to use. For example, the Contemporary Fax template is selected in the figure. The selected template appears in the Preview window on the right side of the New dialog box. Click **OK**.

4 Word displays a new document with placeholder text that helps you get started. What you see is a copy of the template, not the original template. Click the placeholder text and type the text you want to add to the template.

> **NOTE** ▼
>
> To save a document that is based on a template, choose the File Save command and save the document as you would any other.

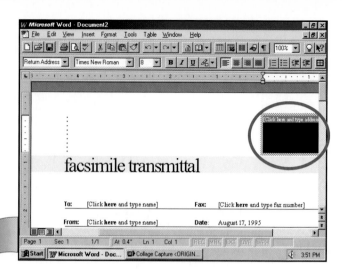

5 If you don't want to use the template you selected, abandon the document. To do so, click **File** in the menu bar and click **Close**. Choose **No** to abandon the document. ■

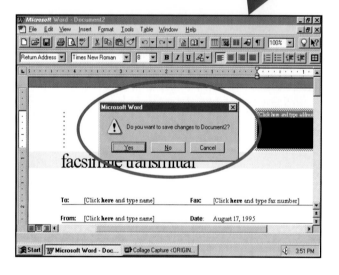

Using a Wizard

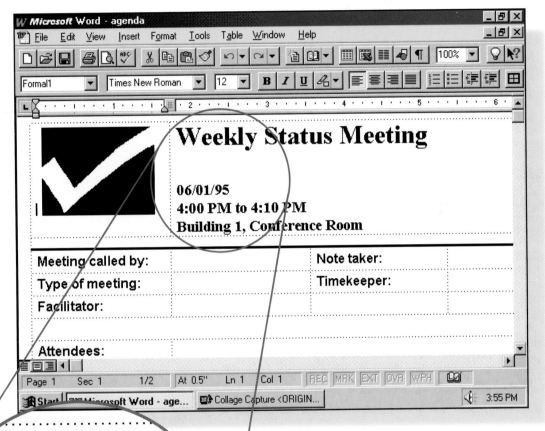

"Why would I do this?"

There are several special templates called template wizards that you can use to create a new document. A template wizard walks you through the process of creating a document using dialog boxes. You can create the following types of documents: agendas, awards, calendars, resumés, fax cover sheets, legal pleading papers, letters, memos, newsletters, and tables. Just choose the wizard you want, and you get a running start on creating a professional-looking document.

83

1 Click **File** in the menu bar. Then click **New**. You see the New dialog box.

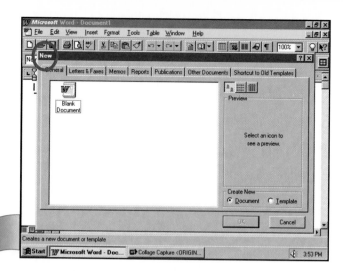

2 Click the **Other Documents** folder tab. Then select the icon for the wizard you want to start, and it appears in the Preview box. Click **OK**.

3 Word displays a wizard dialog box. Follow the steps in each wizard dialog box that appears to create your new document. After you finish creating the document, save it using the File Save command. ■

WHY WORRY?

If you don't want to create a new document using the wizard, abandon it by choosing Cancel in a wizard dialog box.

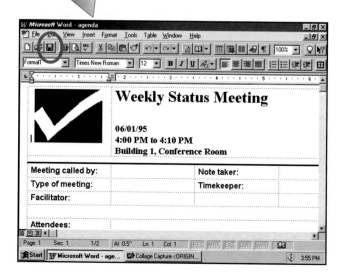

PART IV

Formatting Your Document

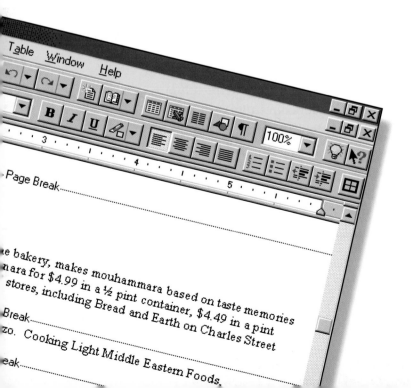

Formatting the document means to change the appearance of text in your document. Using Word for Windows' formatting tools, you can make your document more attractive and readable.

Making text bold is one of the most common formatting changes you'll make in a document. Adding italics is another common formatting change. The "Sample Documents" section (Part X) contains several documents that use boldface and italics.

The Underline command enables you to underline text in your document. To underline text, you can use the Format Font command and then choose from several underline styles in the Font dialog box. The Underline styles include single, words only, double, and dotted. In this part, you learn how to apply the underline styles using the mouse.

A *font* is a style of type in a particular typeface and size. Word for Windows displays various fonts and font sizes in the Formatting toolbar. You can use the fonts provided by Word for Windows as well as fonts designed especially for your printer. If Word for Windows does not have a screen version of the printer font you select, it substitutes a font. In this case, the printout looks different from the screen. The "Sample Documents" section (Part X) contains several documents that illustrate the effect of font changes.

You can align text left, center, right, or justified. The default alignment is left. *Left alignment* means that text is aligned flush with the left margin. Center alignment centers text between the left and right margins. Right-aligned text appears flush with the right margin. Justified text spreads text between the left and right margins by expanding or contracting the space between words.

Left-aligned text appears "ragged right" on the page or column, which is easy to read. Usually, left-alignment is used for conventional and office correspondence. Justified text, which has an orderly look, is generally used in multiple-column newsletters, newspapers, and magazines.

The "Sample Documents" section (Part X) contains a few documents that use center and right alignment. If you want to justify text, select the text you want to justify. Then simply click the Justify button on the Formatting toolbar.

Word for Windows provides another way to align paragraphs. You can indent paragraphs from the left, right, or both margins. You can also indent only the first line of the paragraph, or you can leave the first line flush left and indent all the others.

With the Bullets and Numbering command, you can choose the type of bullet that you want to insert in a bulleted list. You can also choose the type of numbering scheme you want to use in a numbered list. The numbering feature will automatically remember your list to accommodate additional entries. Word for Windows' automatic formatting feature lets you create bulleted and numbered lists as you type.

Setting tabs can be tricky. You choose the Format Tabs command and specify tab stops in the Tabs dialog box. In this part, you learn the easy way to set tab stops for the entire document using the ruler. You can also change the tab stops for just one paragraph.

When you choose the File Page Setup command, you will see the Page Setup dialog box, which contains four types of options: Margins, Paper Size, Paper Source, and Layout. You can move from one set of options to another by clicking the appropriate tab in the Page Setup dialog box.

The Margins options in the Page Setup dialog box control the top, bottom, left, and right margins. The Paper Size options control the paper size (width and height) of the paper you print on and the orientation. The default print orientation is portrait, which means that the document prints vertically on the paper. You can choose Landscape to print the document sideways or horizontally on the paper. If the document is too wide, you can try moving some text if possible, or make the font size smaller. If the document is still too large to print on one page, you can change the top, bottom, left, and right margins. You also might consider reducing the printout using the Shrink to Fit option in the Print Preview screen. This option eliminates lagging single lines on a page (called orphans and widows). It is a good idea to experiment with all the page setup options until you get the results you want. See Part VIII, "Viewing and Printing Documents," for more information on the Print Preview command.

Normally, documents are single-spaced. However, Word for Windows enables you to change the line spacing in your documents. You can choose from Single, 1.5 lines, Double, At Least (the current point size), Exactly, and Multiple. The At Least line spacing option specifies the minimum amount of space between lines. Word for Windows adds additional space as needed. The Exactly option specifies a fixed amount of space between lines. In Exact Mode, Word for Windows does not add additional space, even if needed. Multiple specifies an increased or decreased amount of space between lines (in points or lines). The "Sample Documents" section (Part X) contains a document that uses double-spacing.

Bold

Italic

<u>Underline</u>

Making Text Bold, Italic, and Underlined

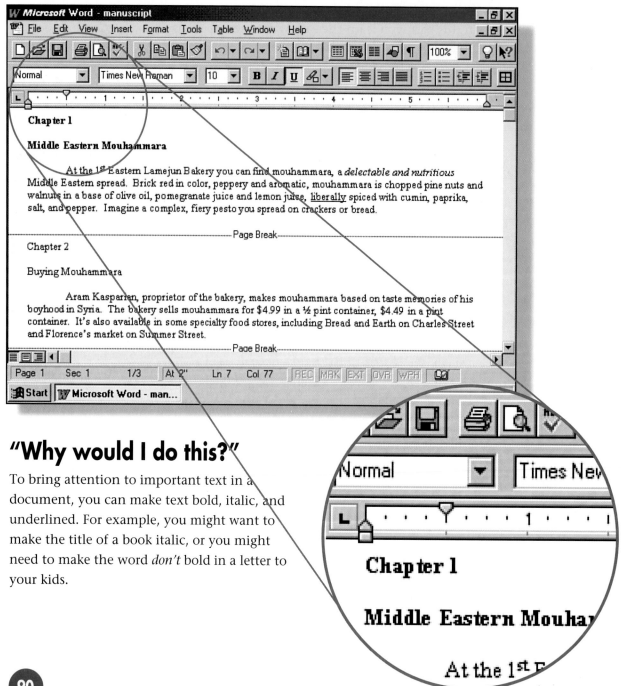

"Why would I do this?"

To bring attention to important text in a document, you can make text bold, italic, and underlined. For example, you might want to make the title of a book italic, or you might need to make the word *don't* bold in a letter to your kids.

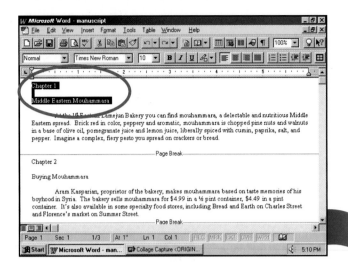

1 Click in the left margin next to *Chapter 1*, hold down the mouse button, and drag down to the next line *Middle Eastern Mouhammara*. This selects the two lines of the text you want to make bold.

2 Click the **Bold** button (the button with the 'B' on it) on the Formatting toolbar. Clicking the Bold button applies bold to the selected text—in this case, the chapter titles.

> **NOTE** ▼
>
> You can also press Ctrl+B to select the Bold command.

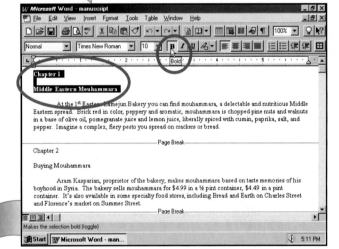

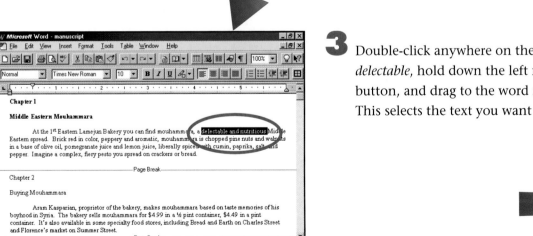

3 Double-click anywhere on the word *delectable*, hold down the left mouse button, and drag to the word *nutritious*. This selects the text you want to italicize.

4 Click the **Italic** button (the button with an italicized 'I' on it) on the Formatting toolbar. Clicking the Italic button italicizes the text—in this case, the words *delectable and nutritious*.

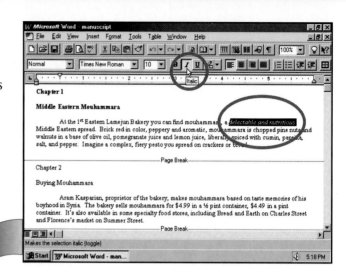

NOTE ▼

You can also press Ctrl+I to select the Italic command.

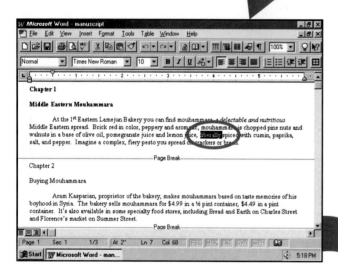

5 Double-click anywhere on the word *liberally*. This selects the text you want to underline.

WHY WORRY?

To undo the bold, italic, or underline font styles, click the Undo button on the Standard toolbar immediately after applying the format.

6 Click the **Underline** button on the Formatting toolbar. Clicking the Underline button underlines the text—in this case, the word *liberally*. Click outside the selected text to deselect the text. ■

NOTE ▼

You can also press Ctrl+U to select the Underline command.

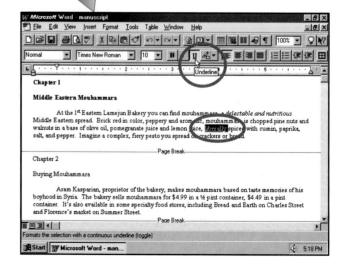

Changing the Font and Font Size

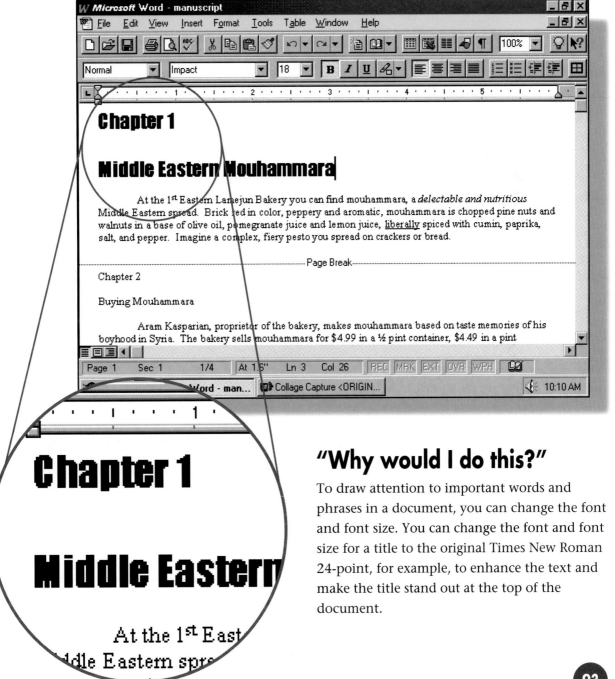

"Why would I do this?"

To draw attention to important words and phrases in a document, you can change the font and font size. You can change the font and font size for a title to the original Times New Roman 24-point, for example, to enhance the text and make the title stand out at the top of the document.

1 Click in the left margin next to *Chapter 1* and drag down to the next line *Middle Eastern Mouhammara*. This selects the text you want to change.

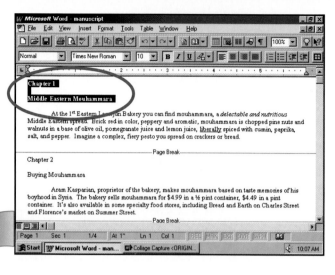

2 Click the down arrow button next to the Font box on the Formatting toolbar. This displays the list of fonts.

3 Click any font in the list. We chose Impact. This changes the font for the selected text.

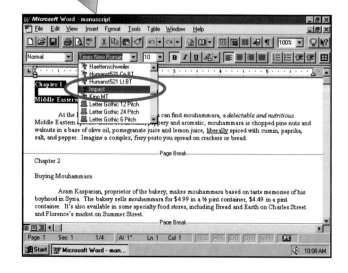

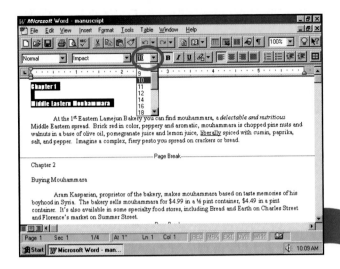

4 Click the down arrow button next to the Font Size box on the Formatting toolbar. This displays the list of font sizes.

NOTE ▼

The font sizes in the list can vary, depending on your printer and the selected font.

5 Click a larger font size (a higher number). We chose 18. This changes the font size for the chapter titles.

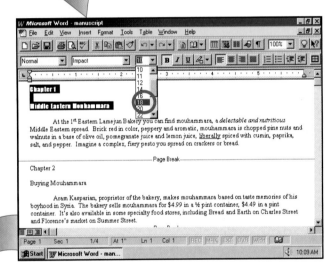

6 Click outside the selected text to deselect the text. The text size increases according to your change. ■

WHY WORRY?

To undo the font size change, immediately click the Undo button in the Standard toolbar.

Centering and Right-Aligning Text

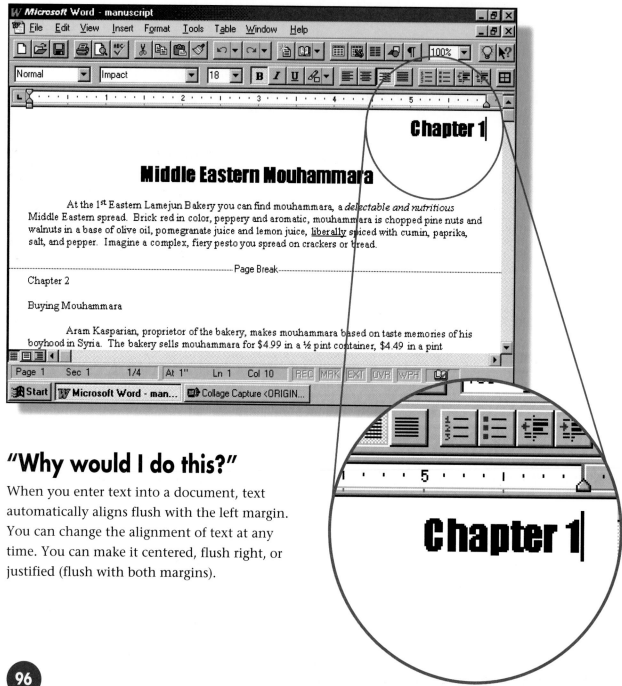

"Why would I do this?"

When you enter text into a document, text automatically aligns flush with the left margin. You can change the alignment of text at any time. You can make it centered, flush right, or justified (flush with both margins).

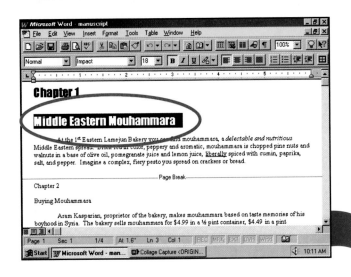

1 Click in the left margin next to *Middle Eastern Mouhammara*. This selects the line of the text you want to center.

2 Click the **Center** button on the Formatting toolbar. This selects the Center command. Word for Windows centers the text—in this case, the chapter title.

WHY WORRY?

To undo the most recent alignment change, click the Undo button on the Standard toolbar.

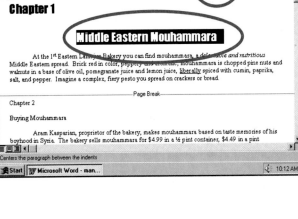

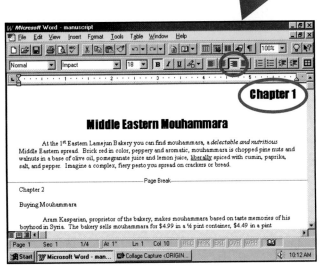

3 Click in the left margin next to *Chapter 1*. This selects the text you want to right-align. Click the **Align Right** button on the Formatting toolbar. Word for Windows right-aligns the title. Click outside the selected text to deselect the text. ■

NOTE ▼

You can also press Ctrl+E to center or Ctrl+R to right-align a paragraph of text.

Indenting Text and Creating a Hanging Indent

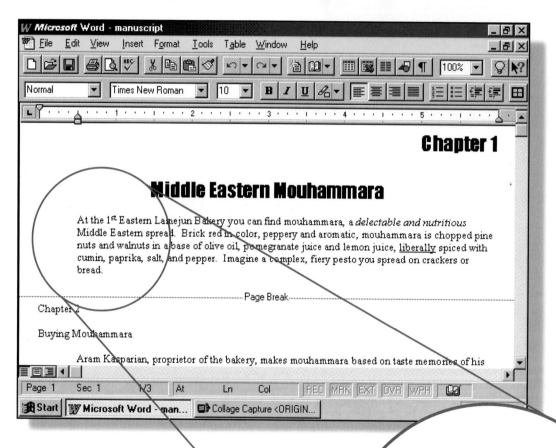

"Why would I do this?"

You can indent an entire paragraph to the right of the left margin to make it stand out. A contract, for example, may contain indented paragraphs. A *hanging indent* "hangs" the first line of a paragraph to the left of the rest of it. Hanging indents are useful for bulleted or numbered lists and bibliographic entries.

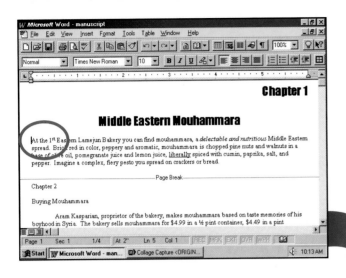

1 Click before the *A* in *At* in the paragraph on page 1. Then press **Backspace** to remove the tab. As you can see, the insertion point is already in the paragraph you want to indent.

2 Click the **Increase Indent** button on the Formatting toolbar. Clicking the Increase Indent button indents text 1/4 inch. As you can see, the paragraph is now indented.

NOTE

You can also press Ctrl+M to indent the current paragraph 1/4 inch. Press Ctrl+Shift+M, click the Undo button, or click the Decrease Indent button to undo the indent.

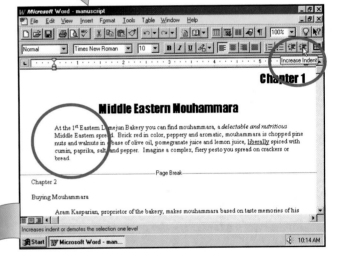

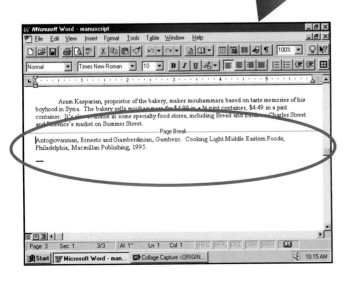

3 To create a hanging indent, click at the beginning of the first line on page 3. Then type **Antogiovannian, Ernesto and Giamberadinian, Gambezo. Cooking Light Middle Eastern Foods, Philadelphia; Macmillan Publishing, 1995.** Press **Enter** twice. Click before the *A* in *Antogiovannian*. This places the insertion point where you want to indent text.

4 Click **Format** on the menu bar. Then click **Paragraph**. Word displays the Paragraph dialog box. This dialog box has two tabs. The first tab, Indents and Spacing, controls the alignment and spacing.

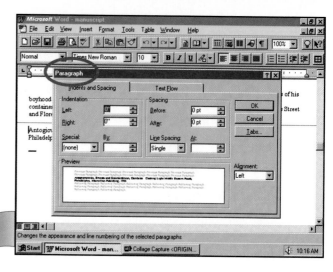

5 Click the down arrow next to the Special option. This displays a list of special indent types. Click **Hanging** to select a hanging indent. The amount to indent by (0.5") is filled in automatically. Click **OK** to confirm the choice and close the dialog box.

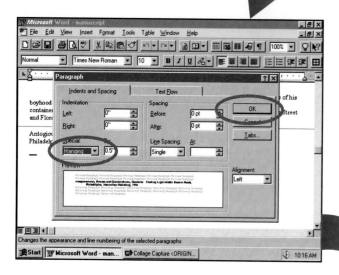

NOTE ▼

You can also press Ctrl+T to create a hanging indent. Press Ctrl+Shift+T or click the Undo button to undo the hanging indent.

6 The first line of the paragraph is flush left, but the second line is indented 1/2 inch. ■

NOTE ▼

You can create hanging indents for several paragraphs at one time. To create hanging indents for more than one paragraph, select those paragraphs first.

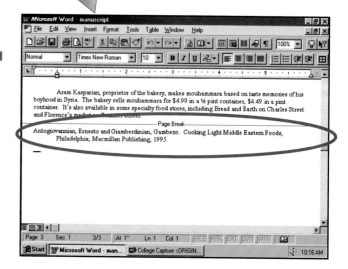

Creating Bulleted and Numbered Lists

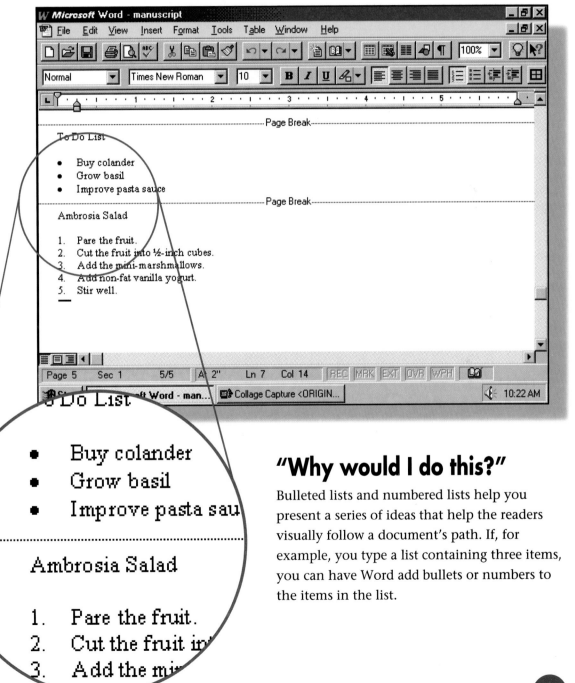

"Why would I do this?"

Bulleted lists and numbered lists help you present a series of ideas that help the readers visually follow a document's path. If, for example, you type a list containing three items, you can have Word add bullets or numbers to the items in the list.

1 Press **Ctrl+End** or scroll to the bottom of the document. Then press **Ctrl+Enter** to insert a page break.

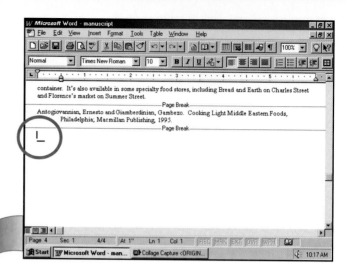

2 On page 4, type the text that appears in the figure so that your computer screen matches the screen shown here.

3 Select all of the paragraphs except the first one. This step selects the text to which you want to add bullets.

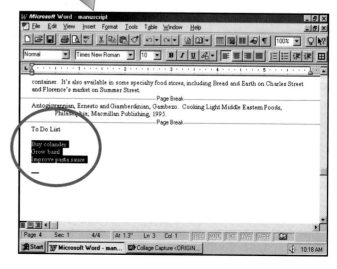

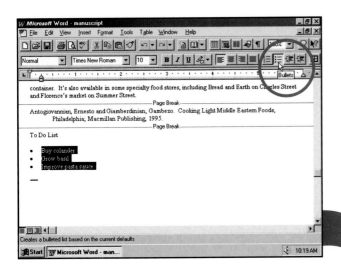

4 Click the **Bullets** button on the Formatting toolbar. Word creates a bulleted list.

5 Click outside the selected text to deselect the text. Now you can see the bulleted list better.

WHY WORRY?

To remove the bullets from the list, immediately click the Undo button on the Standard toolbar.

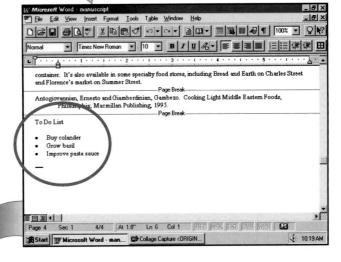

6 Press **Ctrl+End** or scroll to the bottom of the document. Then press **Ctrl+Enter** to insert a page break.

7 On page 5, type the text that appears in the figure so that your computer screen matches the screen shown here.

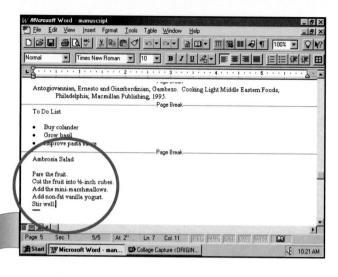

8 Select all of the paragraphs except the first one. This step selects the text that you want to add numbers to.

9 Click the **Numbering** button on the Formatting toolbar. Word creates a numbered list. Click outside the selected text to deselect the text. Now you can see the numbered list better. ■

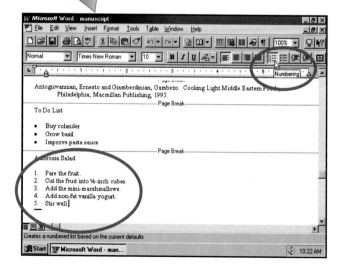

WHY WORRY?

To remove the numbers from the list, immediately click the Undo button on the Standard toolbar.

Setting Tabs and Margins

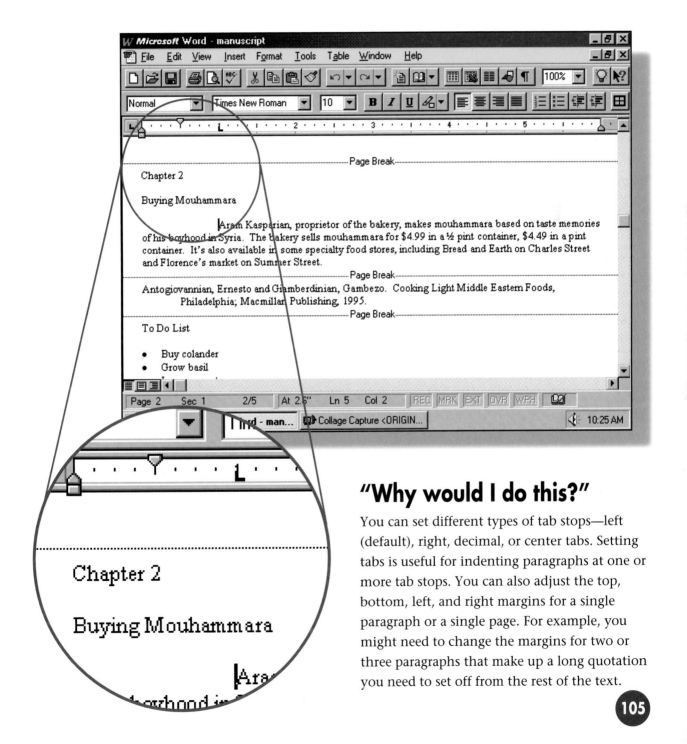

"Why would I do this?"

You can set different types of tab stops—left (default), right, decimal, or center tabs. Setting tabs is useful for indenting paragraphs at one or more tab stops. You can also adjust the top, bottom, left, and right margins for a single paragraph or a single page. For example, you might need to change the margins for two or three paragraphs that make up a long quotation you need to set off from the rest of the text.

1 Click before the *A* in *Aram* at the beginning of the paragraph on page 2. This moves the insertion point to the beginning of the paragraph for which you want to set a tab.

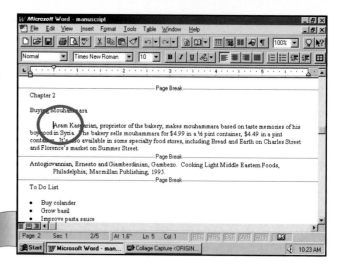

2 If the ruler is not showing at the top of your screen, click **View** in the menu bar and click **Ruler**. Word displays the ruler. At the left edge of the ruler is the Tab Alignment button with the letter **L** on it, which stands for Left tab. You want to set a left tab.

NOTE ▼

Click the Tab Alignment button to choose the type of tab stop—left (default), center, right, or decimal tab.

3 Click beneath the number **1** on the ruler to insert a tab marker (in this case, the letter L) under the number 1.

WHY WORRY?

Word for Windows provides a default tab stop every 1/2 inch.

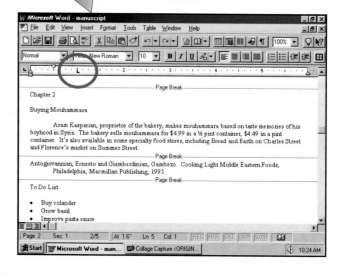

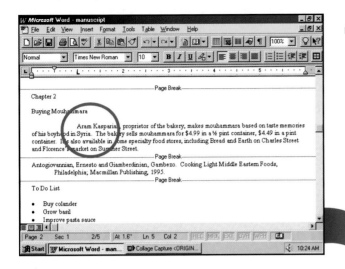

4 Press the **Tab** key to insert a tab and move the insertion point to the next tab stop. As you can see, the first sentence in the paragraph starts one inch from the left margin.

WHY WORRY?

If you want to remove the tab stop, select the text for which you set the tab, point to the tab marker, and drag it off the ruler. Then start over. Or, drag the tab marker to a new location on the ruler.

5 Click **File** in the menu bar and click **Page Setup**. You see the Page Setup dialog box. This dialog box includes four tabs: Margins, Paper Size, Paper Source, and Layout. By default, Margins is displayed. You see text boxes for each of the four margins: Top, Bottom, Left, and Right. The Top entry is selected.

WHY WORRY?

To cancel the margin change, click Cancel in the Page Setup dialog box.

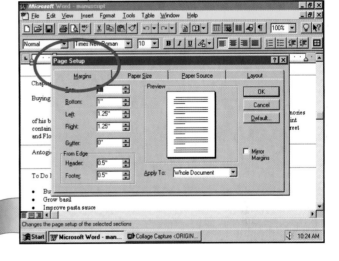

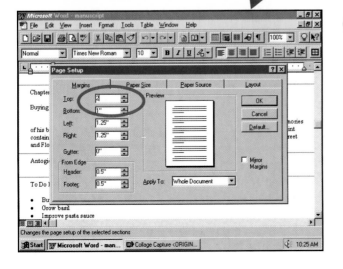

6 Type **2** and click **OK**. This confirms the new margin settings and closes the dialog box. Press **Ctrl+Home** to move the insertion point to the top of the document. The document now has a two-inch top margin. ■

NOTE ▼

The default margins are 1 inch for the top and bottom and 1.25 inches for the left and right.

TASK 33

Double-Spacing a Document

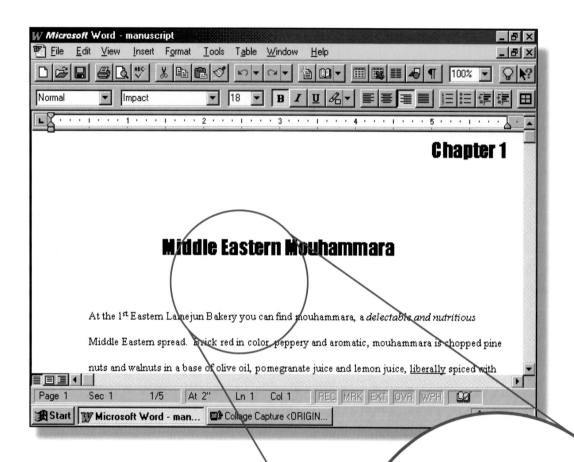

"Why would I do this?"

With Word for Windows, you can adjust line spacing to improve the appearance of a document. The line-spacing options include single-spacing (default), 1-1/2 lines, and double-spacing. For example, you might want to double-space a draft, a manuscript, or a script so that you can mark your changes more easily on the printed pages.

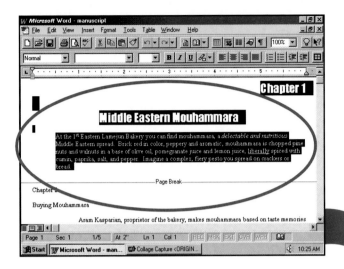

1 Press **Ctrl+Home** to move to the top of the document. Then hold down the mouse button and drag the mouse to select all the text on page 1. This selects the text you want to double-space.

2 Press **Ctrl+2**. Pressing Ctrl+2 tells Word for Windows to double-space the selected text.

> **NOTE** ▼
>
> To specify single-spacing, press Ctrl+1; for 1.5 lines, press Ctrl+5.

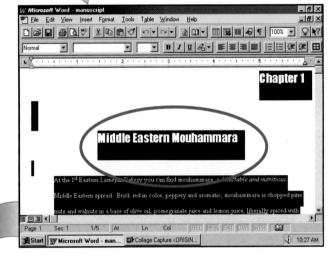

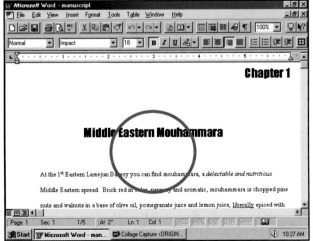

3 Click outside the selected text to deselect the text. As you can see, the text is double-spaced. ■

> **WHY WORRY?**
>
> To undo the line-spacing change, immediately click the Undo button on the Standard toolbar.

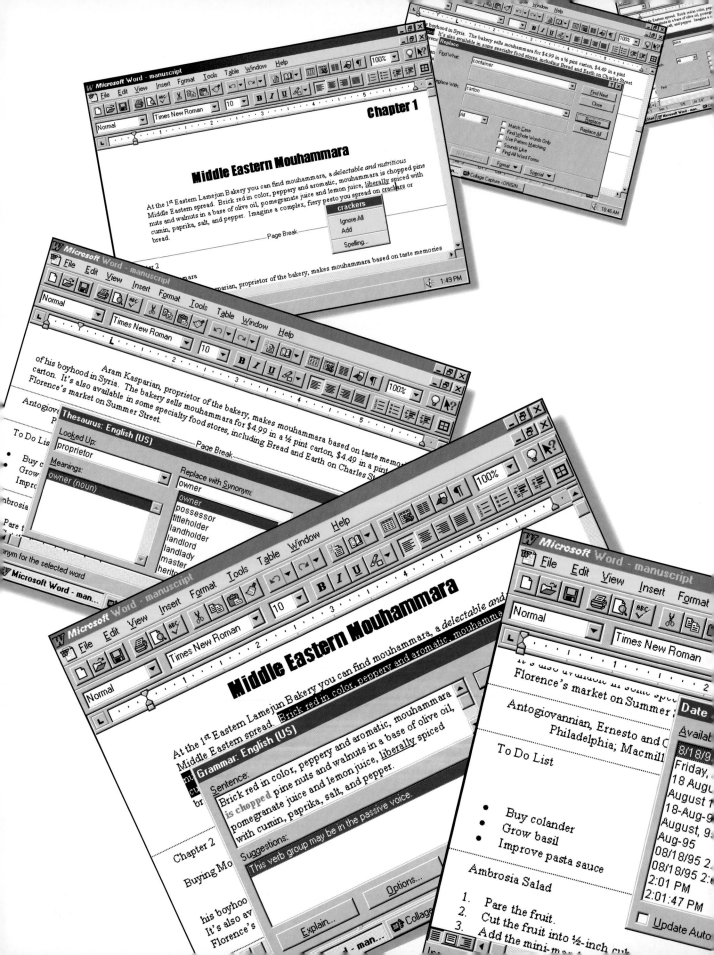

PART V
More Editing

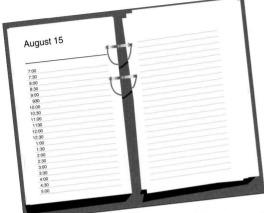

This part shows you how to search for text, find and replace text, check your spelling, use the thesaurus, check your grammar, insert the date, and insert a special character.

The Find command enables you to search for specific text, character formats (such as bold, italic, and underline), or paragraph formats (such as indents and spacing). The text you search for can also include special characters, em and en dashes, manual page breaks, section breaks, carets, and any other special characters that appear in a document. You can search for a string of up to 255 characters.

Word for Windows' Replace feature lets you find anything the Find command does, and then change it to anything else. You can quickly and easily change a word or phrase, character formats, paragraph formats, or any special character throughout the document.

The Find command and the Replace command give you several search options you can use to refine the search.

- The Search option specifies the direction of the search in the document. You can choose All to search the entire document from the insertion point, Down to search forward, or Up to search backward through the document.

- The Match Case option searches for text with the specified combination of upper- and lowercase letters.

- The Find Whole Words Only option searches for whole words only and does not find occurrences of the specified word that are part of other words.

- The Use Pattern Matching option searches for patterns in formatting, such as indented paragraphs or numbered headings.

- The Sounds Like option searches for homonyms—words that sound like the word for which you are currently searching.

- The Find All Word Forms option finds and replaces all forms of a word. For example, you can find the forms of "give" and replace them with forms of "provide." Word finds "give," "gives," "gave," and "giving," and replaces them with "provide," "provides," "provided," and "providing."

With the Spelling feature, you can use custom dictionaries for medical, legal, and technical documents to ensure accuracy when spell-checking special terms for documents in those fields. Word for Windows' AutoCorrect feature automatically checks your spelling as you type. In addition to the Auto-Correct feature described in this part, you can choose the Tools, Spelling command, press F7, or click the Spelling button on the Standard toolbar to run a spell check. A Spelling dialog box appears, giving you several spelling options to choose from. Some of these options appear on the AutoCorrect Spelling shortcut menu.

The Thesaurus is very useful for looking up synonyms and antonyms for words used in your document. A synonym is a word that has a similar meaning. An antonym is a word of opposite meaning.

Word provides another proofreading tool: a grammar checker that checks your document for correct grammar and use of language. You can specify grammar rules and writing style options to customize the grammar checker to meet your specific needs.

Word for Windows' Date and Time feature enables you to enter dates and times in a document to show when you created or last modified the document.

Special characters include fonts such as Symbol and Wingdings, Greek letters, and scientific symbols. *Wingdings* are decorative characters such as bullets, stars, and flowers. You can choose the MS Line Draw font to insert foreign language characters such as tildes (~) and umlauts (¨).

There are two methods for entering special characters:

1. You can use the Symbol dialog box, which shows a keyboard of special characters.

2. You can use a series of special keystrokes that appear in a list when you choose the Special Characters tab in the Symbol dialog box.

This part introduces you to some of Word for Windows' time-saving features for editing data in your documents.

TASK 34

Searching for Text

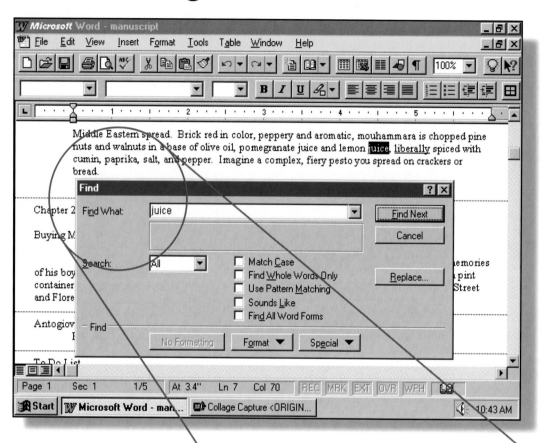

"Why would I do this?"

The Find feature enables you to quickly locate a specific word or phrase, character format, paragraph format, or special character. This feature is handy when you want to find specific text in a document that is many pages long.

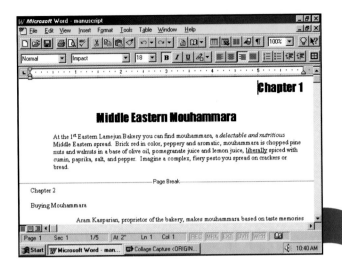

1 Press **Ctrl+Home** to move the insertion point to the beginning of the document. When you begin the search, Word for Windows searches from the location of the insertion point forward.

NOTE ▼

If you start searching when the insertion point is in the middle of the document, Word for Windows searches from that location to the end of the document and then displays a message box that asks whether you want to continue searching from the beginning.

2 Press **Ctrl+F** to open the Find dialog box. The insertion point is in the Find What text box.

NOTE ▼

The Find dialog box includes the Find What text box and other options that control how the program searches the document.

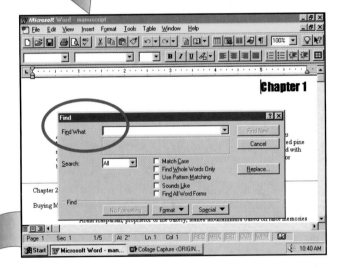

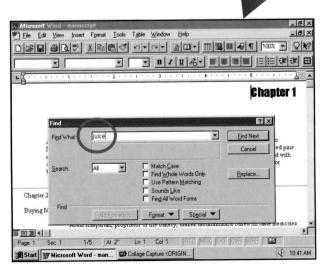

3 Type **juice**. This text, called the *search string*, is what you want to find.

NOTE ▼

By default, Word finds any occurrence of this text, regardless of the case. You can specify that you want to find only whole words and to match case. To do so, click the Find Whole Words Only or Match Case check boxes.

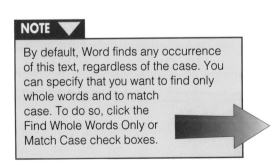

4 Click **Find Next** or press **Alt+F** to select the Find Next button and start the search. Word for Windows finds the first occurrence of the search string and highlights that text. The dialog box remains open on-screen.

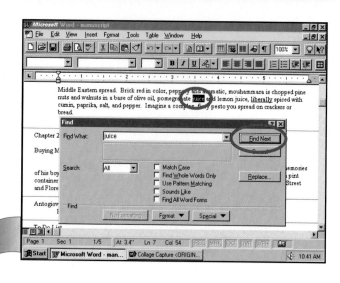

WHY WORRY?

If Word for Windows does not find the text, you see an alert message. Click OK and try the search again. Be sure to type the search string correctly.

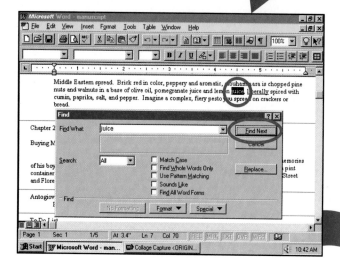

5 Click **Find Next**. This selects the Find Next button again to continue the search. Word for Windows finds the next occurrence of the search string and highlights that text. The dialog box remains open on-screen.

NOTE ▼

If you can't see the text that Word finds, drag the Find dialog box's title bar to uncover the selected text.

6 Click **Cancel** to close the dialog box. ■

NOTE ▼

After you close the dialog box, you can press Shift+F4 to repeat the search.

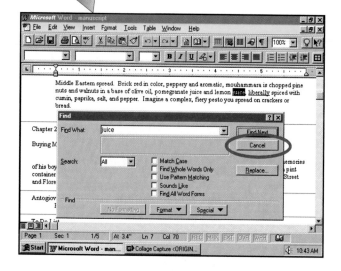

Finding and Replacing Text

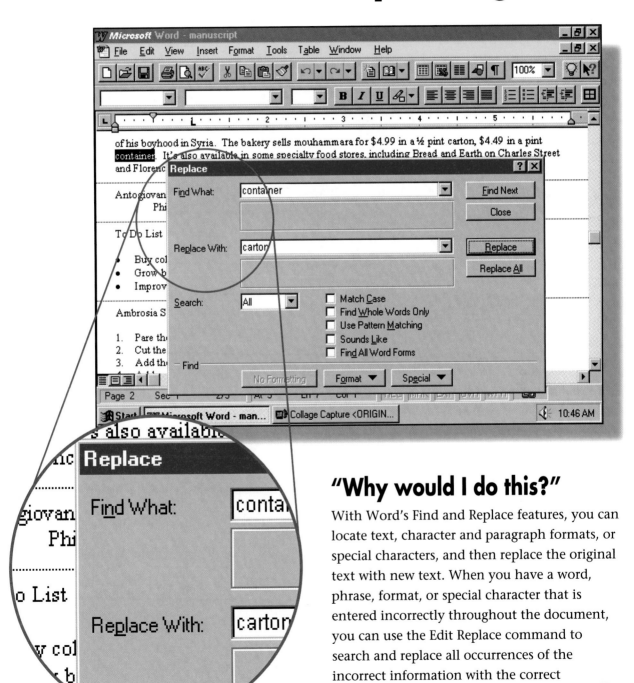

"Why would I do this?"

With Word's Find and Replace features, you can locate text, character and paragraph formats, or special characters, and then replace the original text with new text. When you have a word, phrase, format, or special character that is entered incorrectly throughout the document, you can use the Edit Replace command to search and replace all occurrences of the incorrect information with the correct information.

117

1 Press **Ctrl+Home**. This moves the insertion point to the beginning of the document. When you begin the search, Word for Windows searches from the location of the insertion point forward.

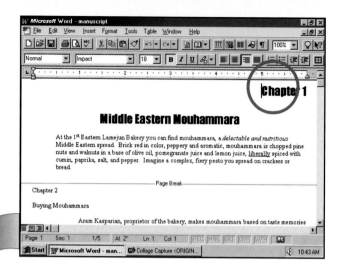

2 Press **Ctrl+H** to open the Replace dialog box. The insertion point is in the Find What text box. Notice the previous search string appears in the Find What box.

NOTE ▼

The Replace dialog box includes the Find What text box, the Replace With text box, and other options that control how the program performs the search and replace operation.

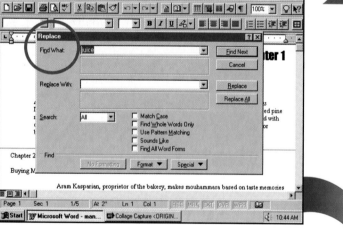

3 Type **container** and press **Tab**. This text, called the *search string*, is what you want to find. Pressing Tab moves the insertion point to the Replace With text box.

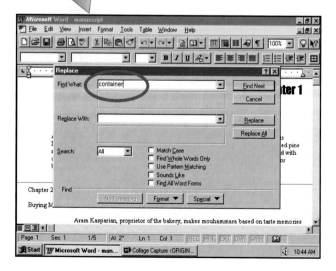

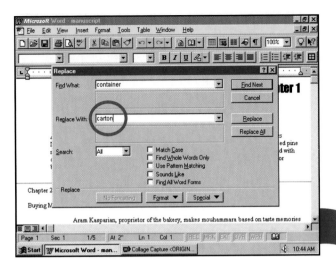

4 Type **carton**. This is the text you want to use as the replacement.

5 Click **Find Next** to start the search. Word for Windows finds the first occurrence of the search string and highlights that text. The dialog box remains open on-screen. (You can move the dialog box to see other text by dragging the dialog box's title bar.)

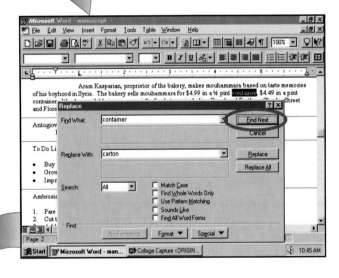

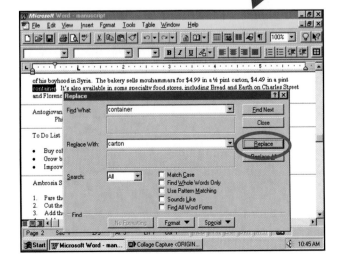

6 Click **Replace**. Word replaces the high-lighted text with the replacement text and then moves to the next occurrence of the search string. The dialog box remains open on-screen. Repeat this step for all occurrences Word finds.

7 When Word finds no more occurrences of the search string, you see an alert box.

NOTE ▼

To replace all occurrences of the text automatically, click the Replace All button. Be careful; make test replacements before you choose Replace All.

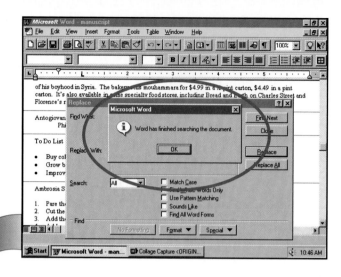

8 Click **OK** to close the alert box. The dialog box remains open.

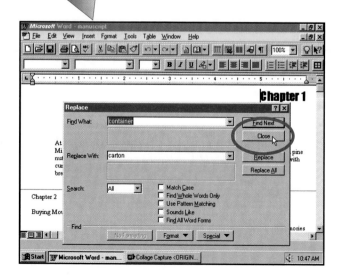

9 Click **Close** to close the dialog box. Now you can see the replaced text. ■

WHY WORRY?

If Word for Windows does not find the text, you see an alert message. Click OK and try the search again. Be sure to type the search string correctly.

Checking Your Spelling

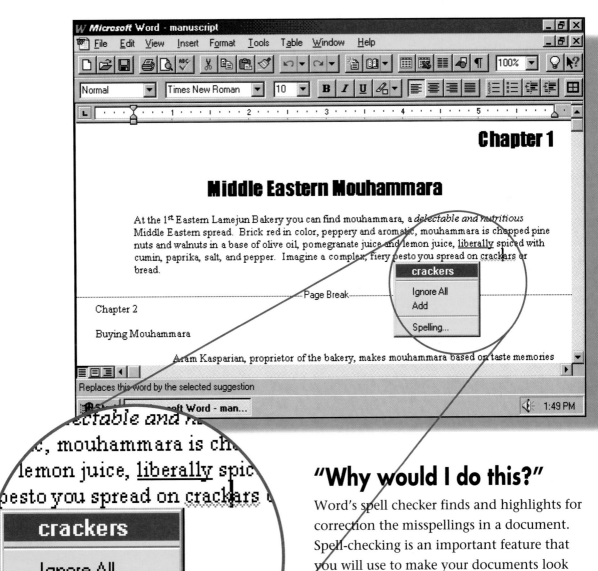

"Why would I do this?"

Word's spell checker finds and highlights for correction the misspellings in a document. Spell-checking is an important feature that you will use to make your documents look professional and letter perfect. Word's Auto-Correct spell checker finds misspelled words automatically as you type them. Keep it turned on to prevent misspellings from occurring.

1 On page 1 in the document in the second sentence, remove the first occurrence of the letter *p* in the word *chopped*. Next, on page 1 in the last sentence, change the *e* in *crackers* to an *a*. Click anywhere in the paragraph. A wavy red line appears beneath each word that contains a spelling error.

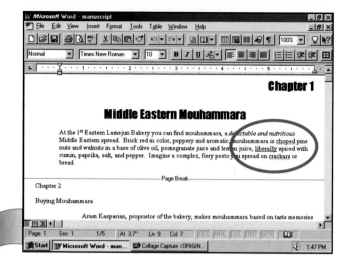

2 Move the mouse pointer to the first wavy red-underlined word and click the right mouse button. The Spelling shortcut menu appears. Choose a word from the suggested spelling list to change the word in the document.

NOTE ▼

The Spelling shortcut menu lists suggested spellings for the word not found in the dictionary. You can select from several spelling options to correct the error.

3 Move the mouse pointer to the next wavy red-underlined word and click the right mouse button. The Spelling shortcut menu appears. Choose a word from the suggested spelling list to change the word in the document. ■

WHY WORRY?

Choose Ignore All to remove the under-line and tell Word for Windows to ignore all occurrences of this word (that is, not to stop on this word again).

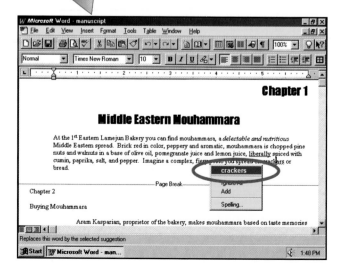

Using the Thesaurus

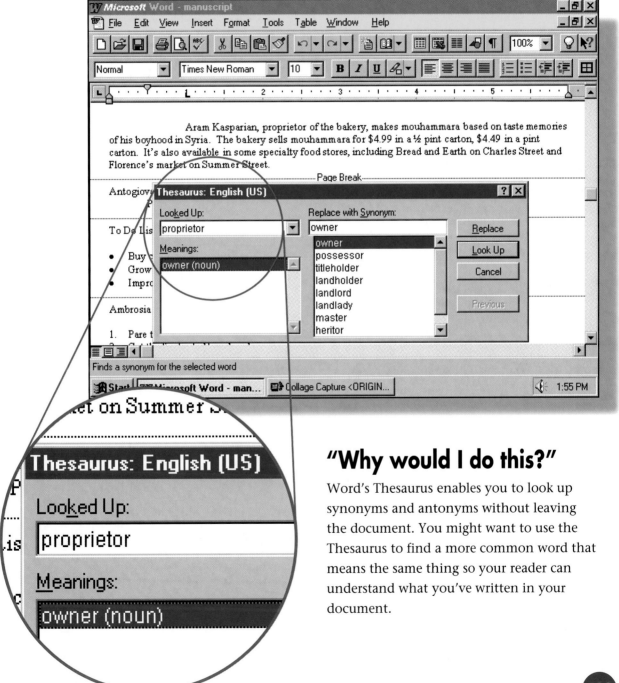

"Why would I do this?"

Word's Thesaurus enables you to look up synonyms and antonyms without leaving the document. You might want to use the Thesaurus to find a more common word that means the same thing so your reader can understand what you've written in your document.

1 On page 2 in the first sentence, click before the word *proprietor*. You can click before the word or within the word you want to look up.

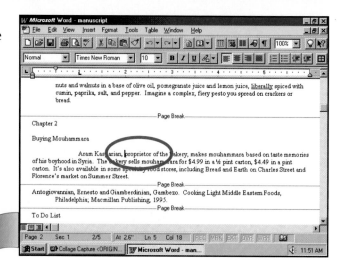

2 Press **Shift+F7** to select the Thesaurus command. You see the Thesaurus dialog box. The Looked Up text box displays the selected word. Beneath this box, you see a list of meanings. To the right of the Looked Up box, you see a list of synonyms.

NOTE ▼

To see additional synonyms, select a synonym in the Replace with Synonym list and click on the Look Up button. Word displays a list of different synonyms.

3 The word *owner* is already selected in the Replace with Synonym list box. Click **Replace** to select the Replace button. Word replaces *proprietor* with *owner* and closes the dialog box. ■

WHY WORRY?

To undo the replacement, click the Undo button on the Standard toolbar immediately.

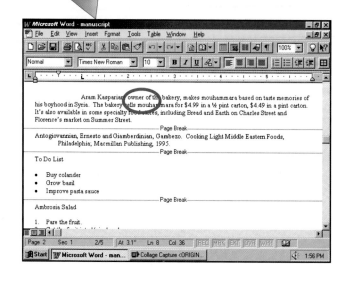

Checking Your Grammar

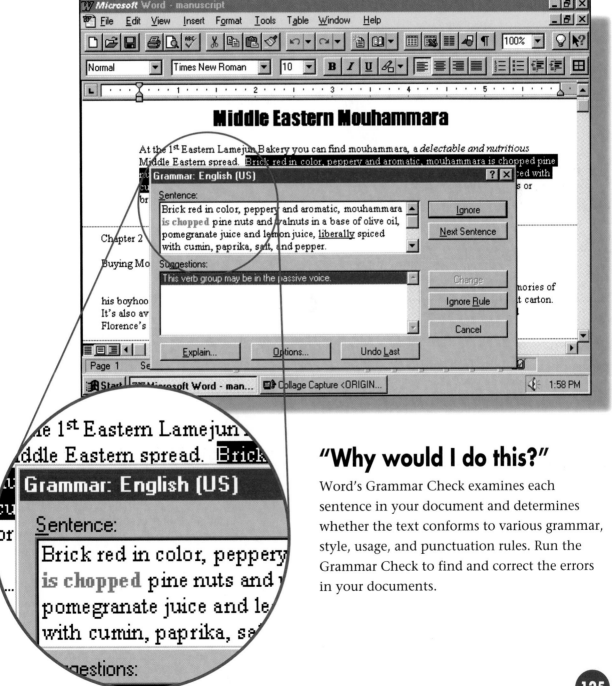

"Why would I do this?"

Word's Grammar Check examines each sentence in your document and determines whether the text conforms to various grammar, style, usage, and punctuation rules. Run the Grammar Check to find and correct the errors in your documents.

1 Press **Ctrl+Home** to start the grammar check at the top of the document.

> **NOTE** ▼
>
> If you start the grammar check when the insertion point is in the middle of the document, Word checks from that location to the end of the document and then displays a message box that asks whether you want to continue checking grammar from the beginning of the document.

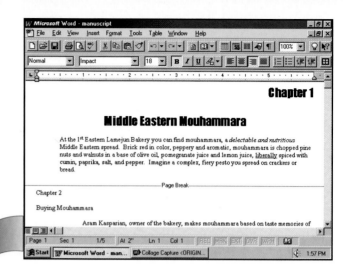

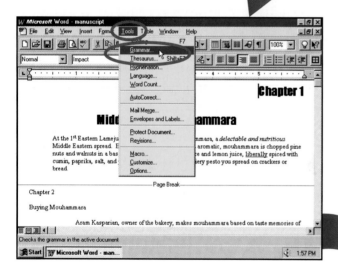

2 Click **Tools** in the menu bar to display the Tools menu. Click **Grammar** to start Grammar Check. Word finds the first error and displays the Grammar dialog box.

3 The sentence that contains the error is highlighted in the document. The errors in grammar are displayed in red in the Sentence box. The advice and an explanation on how to fix the error appear in the Suggestions box. The replacement text appears beneath the suggestion in the Suggestions box, depending on the type of error found in the sentence.

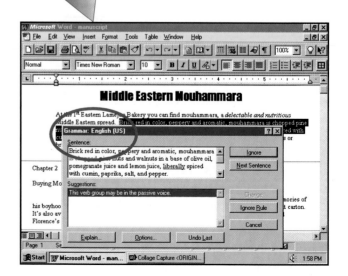

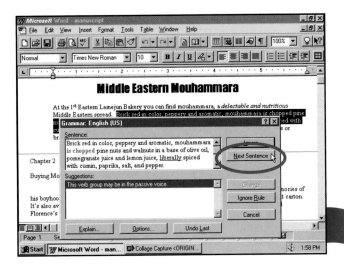

4 Click **Next Sentence**. This option tells Word to skip the current suggestion and check the next sentence.

NOTE ▼

In the Grammar dialog box, you can select from several options. For example, you can choose Ignore to skip the current suggestion and not change the sentence. To correct an error, choose Change to execute the suggestion and change the sentence.

5 When Grammar Check doesn't find any more grammar errors, the Readability Statistics dialog box appears. As you can see, Word displays a window showing the number of words, characters, paragraphs, and sentences in the text, as well as several standard measurements of the document's readability.

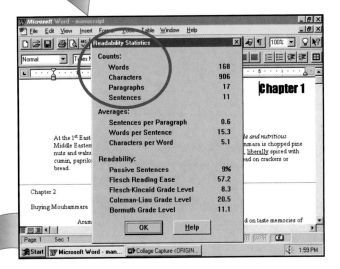

6 Click **OK** to close the Readability Statistics dialog box. ∎

WHY WORRY?

To stop Grammar Check, click Cancel after Word stops on a sentence.

127

TASK 39

Inserting the Date

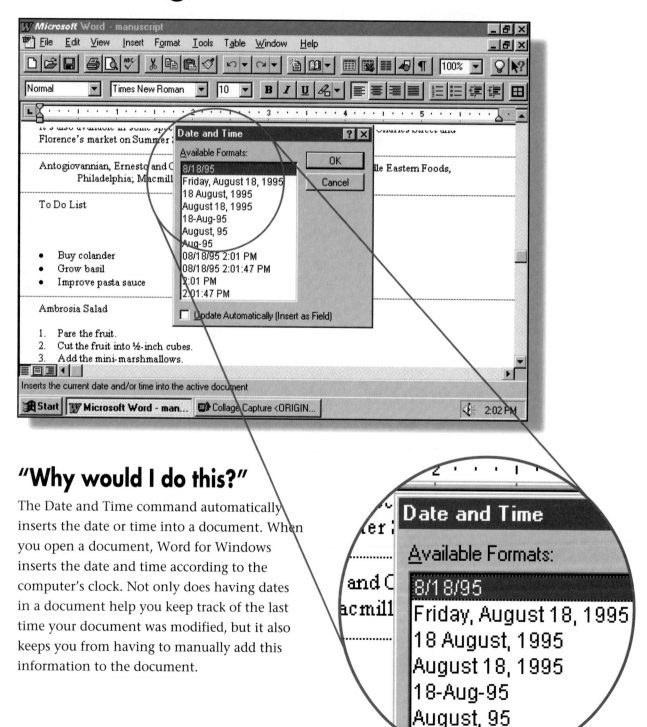

"Why would I do this?"

The Date and Time command automatically inserts the date or time into a document. When you open a document, Word for Windows inserts the date and time according to the computer's clock. Not only does having dates in a document help you keep track of the last time your document was modified, but it also keeps you from having to manually add this information to the document.

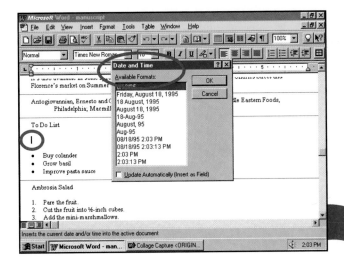

1 Place the insertion point where you want the date to appear. Click **Insert** on the menu bar. Then click **Date and Time**. You see the Date and Time dialog box, which lists the available date and time formats.

NOTE ▼

If the wrong date or time appears, use the Date/Time program in the Windows Control Panel to set the date and time.

2 Click on the fourth highlighted format from the top. This selects the date format. The current date appears in the examples in the dialog box. Click **OK**. Word inserts the date in the document.

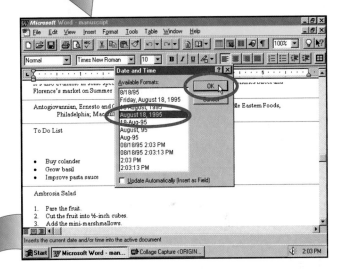

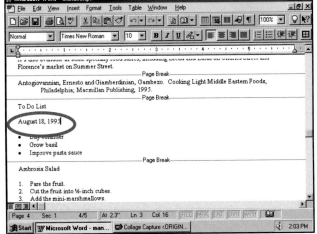

3 You see the current date on-screen. ■

WHY WORRY?

To delete the date, click the Undo button in the Standard toolbar immediately after you insert the date.

Inserting a Special Character

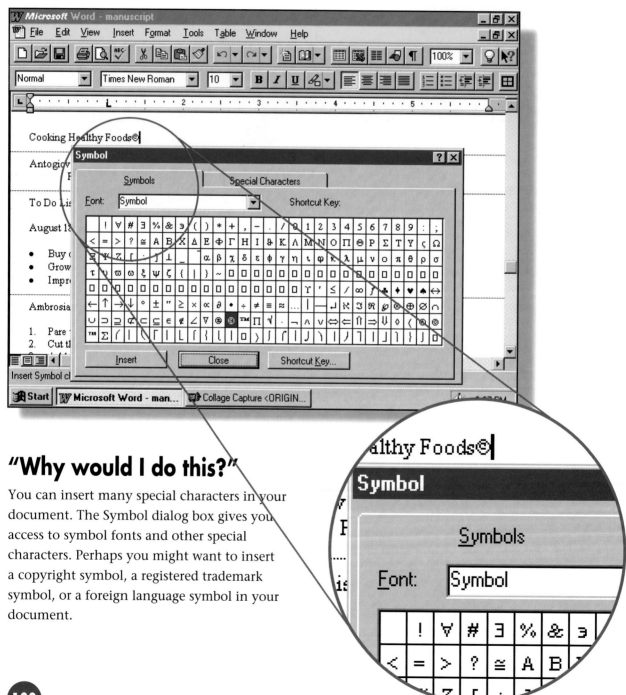

"Why would I do this?"

You can insert many special characters in your document. The Symbol dialog box gives you access to symbol fonts and other special characters. Perhaps you might want to insert a copyright symbol, a registered trademark symbol, or a foreign language symbol in your document.

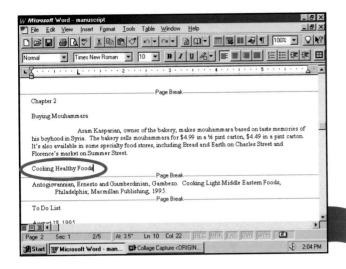

1 Click after *Street* at the end of the paragraph on page 2. Then press **Enter** twice. Next, type **Cooking Healthy Foods**. This enters the title of the book.

2 Click **Insert** in the menu bar. You see a list of Insert commands. Click **Symbol** to select the Symbol command.

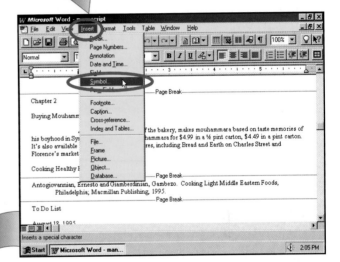

3 You see the Symbol dialog box. This dialog box has two tabs, one for symbols and one for special characters. By default, the Symbols tab is displayed.

4 Click the copyright symbol (©). This selects the symbol you want to insert.

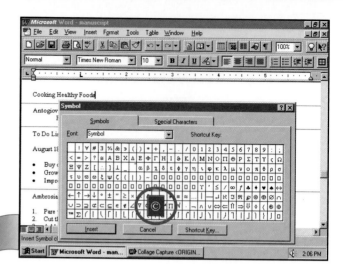

5 Click the **Insert** button. Word for Windows inserts the symbol in your document. Then click **Close** to close the dialog box.

6 The selected symbol appears next to the book title at the insertion point. ■

WHY WORRY?

To undo the insertion, click the Undo button in the Standard toolbar or delete the symbol by pressing Backspace or Delete.

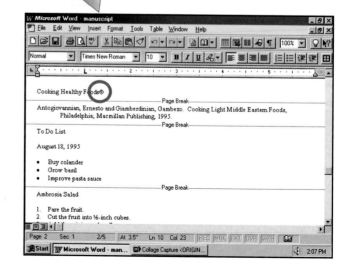

PART VI

More Formatting

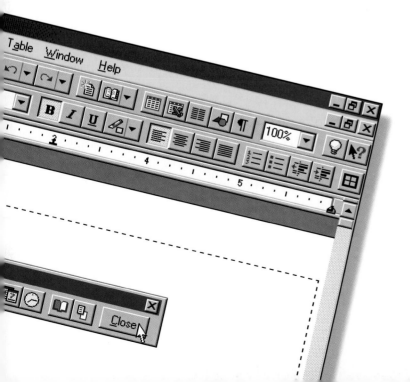

I n this part, you learn how to add a border to a paragraph, shade a paragraph, center a page, number pages, and create and edit headers and footers.

One of the best ways to enhance the appearance of a document is to add borders to the text in the document. You can use the Borders button on the Formatting toolbar to add boxes around paragraphs, add emphasis lines anywhere in the document, and shade paragraphs. Adding a border, lines, and shading works for document headings or sections of a document that you want to distinguish. Adding lines works well on newsletters, for example. Lines can also be used to separate parts of a document. The "Sample Documents" section (Part X) contains several documents that show off these features.

With Word's new automatic borders feature, you can place a border above a paragraph by typing three or more dashes, underscores, or equal signs above a paragraph. Dashes create a thin line, underscores create a thick line, and equal signs create a double line.

When you choose the File Page Setup command, you see the Page Setup dialog box. The Layout options in the Page Setup dialog box include options for sections, headers and footers, vertical alignment, and line numbers. In this part, you learn how to center a page vertically with the vertical alignment option. It is a good idea to experiment with all the layout options until you get the results you want.

When you add page numbers with the Insert Page Numbers command, you add them to a header or footer. You can specify whether to add the page numbers to the top of each page (to a header) or to the bottom of each page (to a footer). You can also specify the alignment.

If you want, you can change the format for the page numbers. Click the Format button in the Page Numbers dialog box, and Word displays the Page Number Format dialog box. From the Number Format list, you can select Arabic numerals (1,2,3...), which is the default, lowercase or uppercase letters, or lowercase or uppercase Roman numerals.

Word lets you add headers and footers to print information at the top and bottom of every page of the printout. You can create your own header and footer information, and you can include any text plus special commands to control the appearance of the header or footer.

If you have a document that is divided into multiple sections, you can define individual headers and footers for each section. Word also lets you create different headers or footers for odd and even pages or for the first page in a document or section. To do so, choose the File, Page Setup command and click the Layout tab. Then you can choose the Headers and Footers options you want.

This part shows you formatting operations you need for enhancing the appearance and layout of your documents.

Adding a Border to a Paragraph

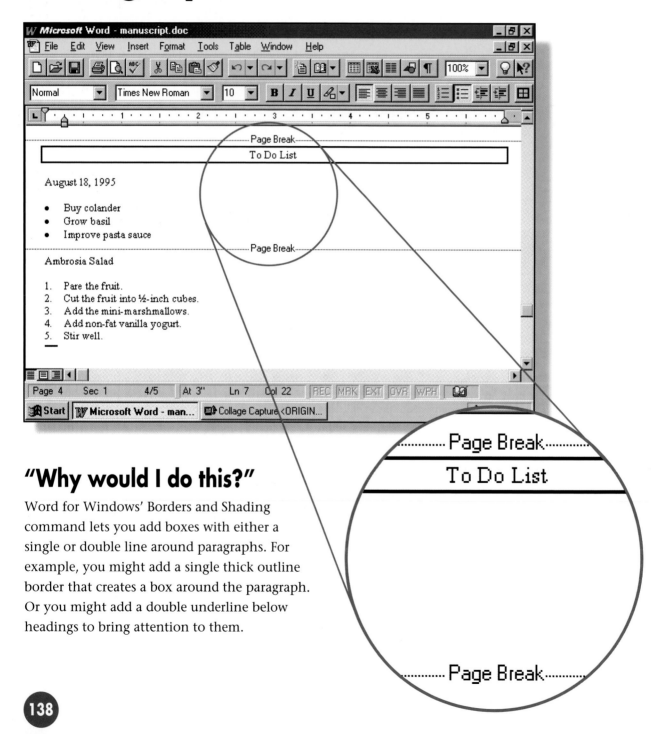

"Why would I do this?"

Word for Windows' Borders and Shading command lets you add boxes with either a single or double line around paragraphs. For example, you might add a single thick outline border that creates a box around the paragraph. Or you might add a double underline below headings to bring attention to them.

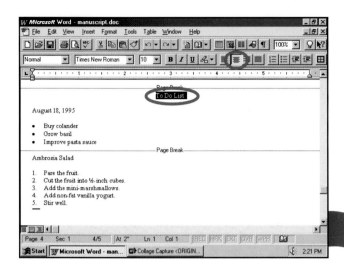

1 Press **PgDn** or scroll down to move to page 4. Select the title *To Do List*. Click the **Center** button on the Standard toolbar to center the text. Leave the text selected so you can add a border to it.

2 Click the **Borders** button at the far right end of the Formatting toolbar. Word displays the Borders toolbar below the Formatting toolbar. The Borders toolbar contains the Line Style list, border samples, and the Shading list.

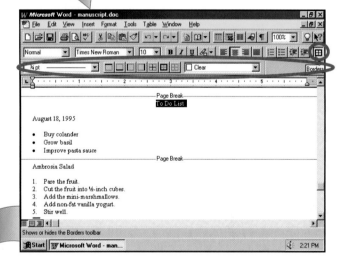

3 Click the down arrow in the Line Style list on the Borders toolbar. A list of lines styles appears. Click **1 1/2 pt** in the Line Style list. This tells Word for Windows what line style you want to use for the border.

4 Click the **Outside Border** button on the Borders toolbar. This tells Word for Windows to outline the edges of the paragraph with a single line.

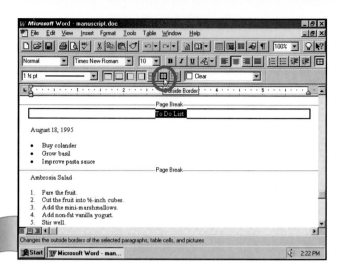

NOTE

You also can add lines at the top, bottom, left, or right side of paragraphs with either a single, double, dashed, or dotted line. Click the Top Border, Bottom Border, Left Border, or Right Border button on the Borders toolbar to tell Word where to place the line.

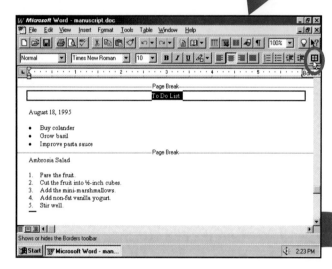

5 Click the **Borders** button on the Formatting toolbar again to hide the Borders toolbar.

6 Click outside the selected text. Word deselects the text, and you can see the outline better. ■

WHY WORRY?

To remove the border, immediately click the Undo button on the Standard toolbar. You also can click the Borders button on the Standard toolbar and click the border placement button that is gray (looks pressed in).

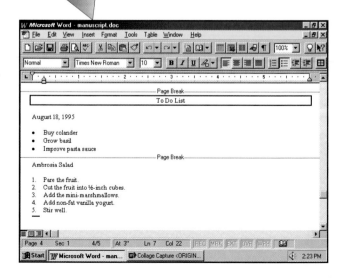

Shading a Paragraph

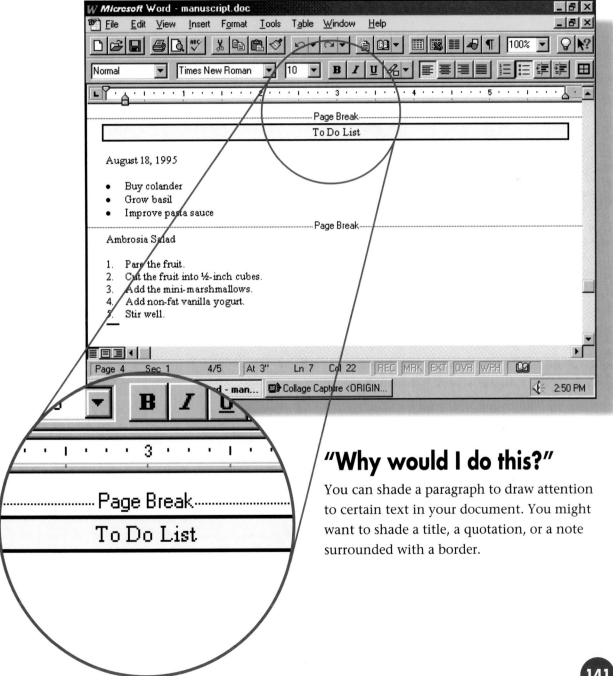

"Why would I do this?"

You can shade a paragraph to draw attention to certain text in your document. You might want to shade a title, a quotation, or a note surrounded with a border.

1 Select the title *To Do List.* This is the paragraph you want to shade.

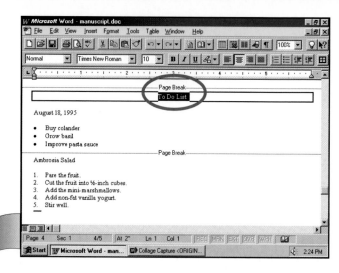

2 Click the **Borders** button on the Formatting toolbar. Word displays the Borders toolbar below the Formatting toolbar. The Borders toolbar contains the Line Style list, border samples, and the Shading list.

3 Click the down arrow in the Shading list on the Borders toolbar. A list of shading patterns appears.

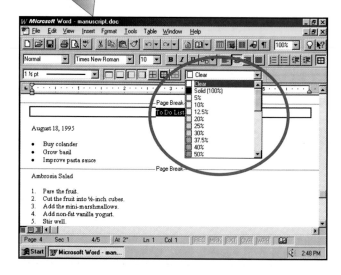

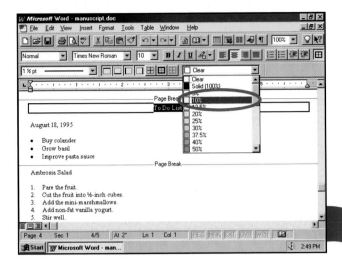

4 Click **10%** in the Shading list. This tells Word for Windows what amount of shading you want.

5 Click the **Borders** button on the Formatting toolbar again to hide the Borders toolbar.

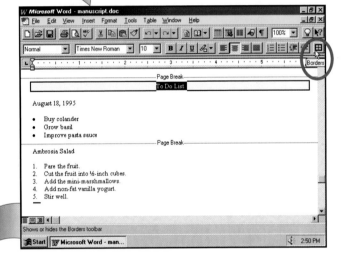

NOTE ▼

Depending on your printer, the shading might print differently than it appears on-screen, or it might not print at all.

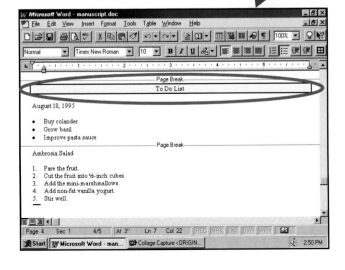

6 Click outside the selected text to deselect it. ■

WHY WORRY?

To remove the shading, immediately click the Undo button on the Standard toolbar. You also can click the Borders button on the Standard toolbar and choose the Clear option in the Shading list.

Centering a Page Vertically

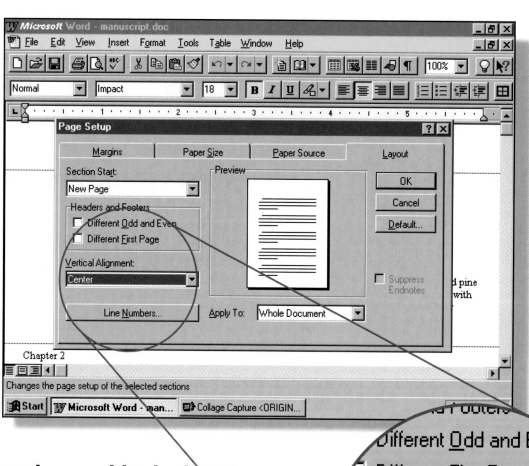

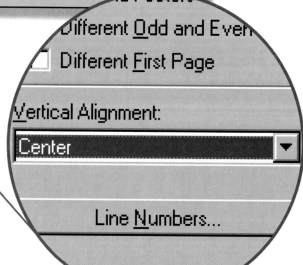

"Why would I do this?"

Word for Windows' Vertical Alignment command enables you to vertically center the text on a page. You can align the text between the top and bottom margins. Centering a page works well for special documents, such as an invitation. Letters often look better on the page when they are centered. Document, chapter, or report titles on a title page also look better when they are centered.

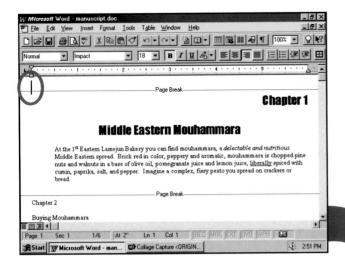

1 Press **Ctrl+Home** or scroll to the top of the document. Then press **Ctrl+Enter** to insert a page break, and press the up arrow key (↑) to move the insertion point to page 1.

2 Type **Cooking Healthy Foods**. Click the **Center** button on the Formatting toolbar to center the text you typed.

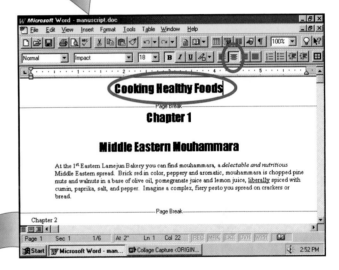

3 Click **File** on the menu bar and click **Page Setup**. Then click the **Layout** tab to display the Layout options in the Page Setup dialog box.

145

4 Click the down arrow next to the **Vertical Alignment** option. This displays a drop-down list of alignment choices.

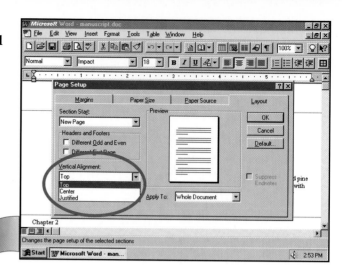

5 Click **Center**. This tells Word for Windows to center the current page.

WHY WORRY?

To cancel the vertical alignment change, click Cancel in the Page Setup dialog box. Or immediately click the Undo button in the Standard toolbar.

6 Click **OK**. Word for Windows closes the Page Setup dialog box. On-screen, you cannot see the vertical alignment change. To do so, you must preview the document. Click on the **Preview** button (the button with a piece of paper and magnifying glass). Click the **Close** button in the Preview window to close it. ■

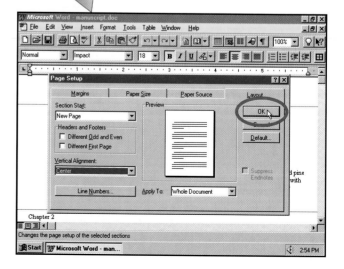

Numbering Pages

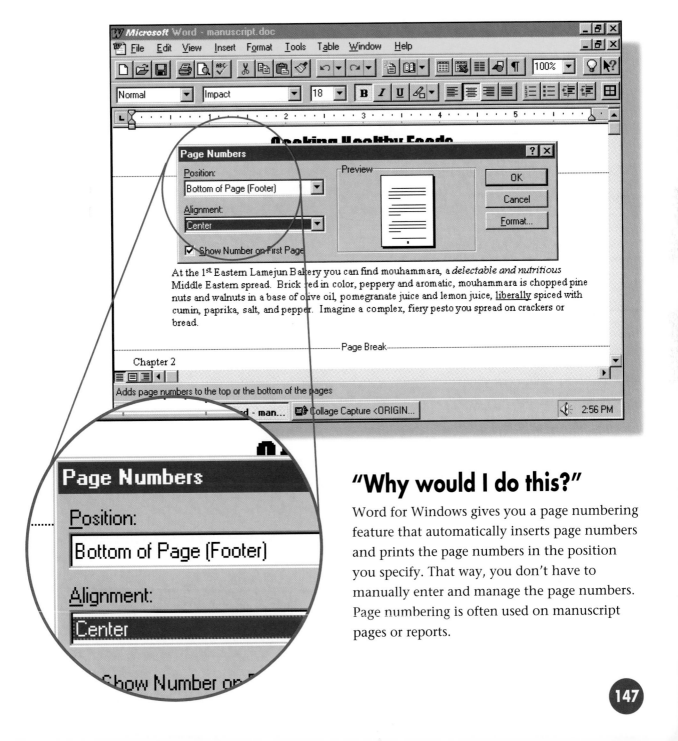

"Why would I do this?"

Word for Windows gives you a page numbering feature that automatically inserts page numbers and prints the page numbers in the position you specify. That way, you don't have to manually enter and manage the page numbers. Page numbering is often used on manuscript pages or reports.

1 Click **Insert** on the menu bar. Then click **Page Numbers**. Word opens the Page Numbers dialog box. The default position for page numbers is Bottom of Page (Footer), and the default alignment is Right.

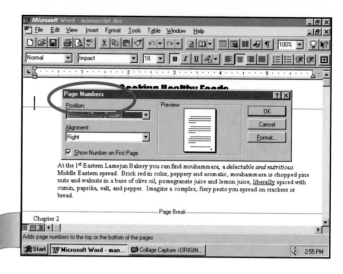

2 Click the down arrow next to the **Alignment** option. This displays a drop-down list of alignment choices. Choose **Center**. This tells Word for Windows to center the page number on every page.

NOTE ▼

If you don't want a page number on the first page, click in the Show Numbers on First Page check box to remove the X from the box.

3 Click **OK**. Word for Windows creates a footer and adds the center-aligned page number to the footer. On-screen, you cannot see the page numbers. To do so, you must preview the document or change to Page Layout view. ∎

WHY WORRY?

If you change your mind, click Cancel in the Page Numbers dialog box or click the Undo button immediately.

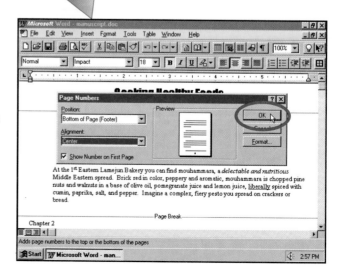

TASK 45

Creating and Editing Headers and Footers

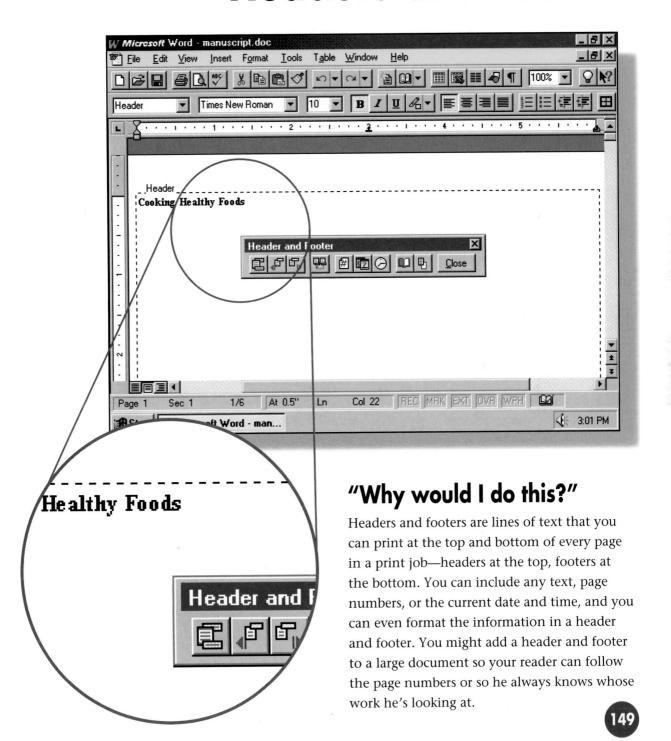

"Why would I do this?"

Headers and footers are lines of text that you can print at the top and bottom of every page in a print job—headers at the top, footers at the bottom. You can include any text, page numbers, or the current date and time, and you can even format the information in a header and footer. You might add a header and footer to a large document so your reader can follow the page numbers or so he always knows whose work he's looking at.

1 Click **View** on the menu bar. Then click **Header and Footer**. Word displays the Header and Footer areas on-screen. You also see the Header and Footer toolbar.

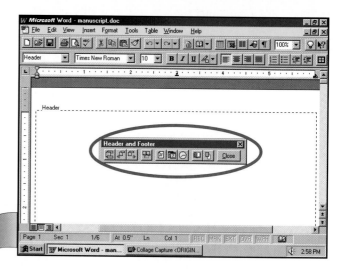

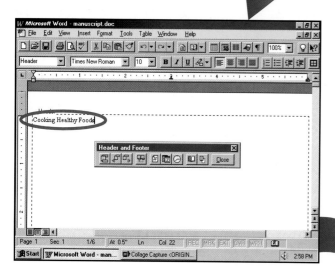

2 Type **Cooking Healthy Foods** in the Header area. This is the text you want to print at the top of each page. (If necessary, drag the Header and Footer toolbar by its title bar to a different area of the document so you can see the Header area.)

3 Click the **Switch Between Header and Footer** button at the left end of the Header and Footer toolbar. This moves the insertion point to the Footer area.

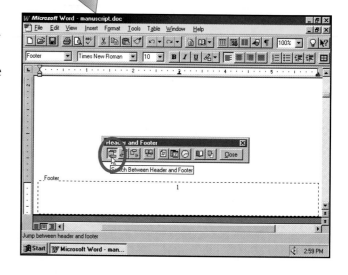

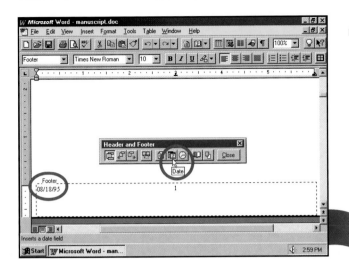

4 Click the **Date** button on the Header and Footer toolbar. This inserts the current date into the Footer area; the date will print at the bottom of each page.

NOTE

You can also insert the page number. Word provides several header and footer options for formatting the header or footer text. These options include bold, italic, underline, different fonts and font sizes, and text alignment.

5 Click the **Switch Between Header and Footer** button on the Header and Footer toolbar to switch back to the Header area. Select the book title text. Then click the **Bold** button on the Formatting toolbar. This adds bold to the text. Click anywhere in the Header area to deselect the text.

NOTE

If you don't want to use a header or footer, select the text in the Header or Footer area and press Delete.

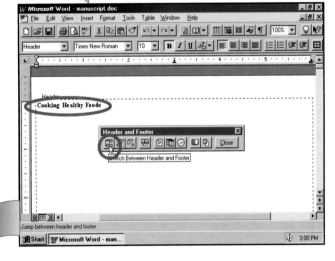

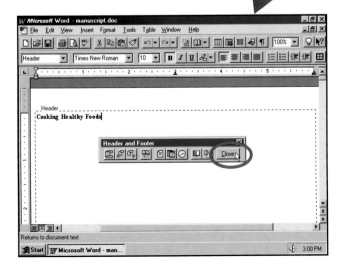

6 Click **Close** in the Header and Footer toolbar to confirm the header and footer and close the Header window. On-screen, you cannot see the header and footer. To do so, you must preview the document or switch to Page Layout view. ■

WHY WORRY?

If something unexpected prints at the top or bottom of your document, check the Header or Footer area.

PART VII
Enhancing Your Document

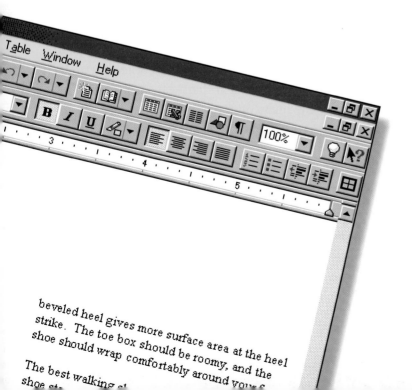

beveled heel gives more surface area at the heel strike. The toe box should be roomy, and the shoe should wrap comfortably around your f

The best walking sl
shoe st

This part shows you how to insert a graphic, move and resize a graphic, and delete a graphic. You also learn how to create a table, enter text in a table, add a row to a table, and delete a row from a table. Finally, you learn how to create a two-column document, type text into a two-column document, and insert a WordArt object.

You can insert graphics to spice up your document. Word for Windows provides clip-art files and supports many import file types and various graphics formats. A Word for Windows graphic image file includes the extension WMF, which stands for Windows Metafiles. You can insert a graphic image that you created with Word's Drawing feature or a graphic created in another program.

Word treats a graphic as an object you can move and resize. You can select the graphic and then move it to a new location in your document, or you can stretch or shrink the graphic to any shape and size you want. If you no longer want the graphic in your document, you can delete the graphic.

The Table feature enables you to instantly create a table with columns and rows. Then you can enter text and numbers (similar to a spreadsheet) in the table without defining tab settings. Once you create the table, you can easily insert and delete rows in the table to suit your needs.

There are several other things you can do to customize a table. You can join cells, split cells, and hide or show gridlines in a table. You can even sort text and numbers in a table, create formulas to perform math calculations on numbers in a table, or import a spreadsheet file into a table.

In this part, you learn how to create two-column documents, which are similar to newspaper-style columns. Newspaper-style columns are sometimes referred to as *snaking* columns. Snaking columns contain text that wraps from the bottom of one column to the top of the next column. Two-column documents are handy for newspapers, newsletters, bulletins, magazine articles, lists, and indexes.

Once you create the two-column document, you learn how to enter text into the two columns. As you type the text, Word for Windows wraps the text within the column until you reach the bottom of the page, and then it wraps the text to the top of the next column.

Word for Windows' Format Columns command enables you to change the column definition of your columns. For example, you can change the number of columns, the space between columns, the width of the columns, and other options in the Columns dialog box. You can also move around columns with the cursor movement keys, as well as copy, move, and delete columns.

This part shows you enhancement techniques you can use to embellish your documents.

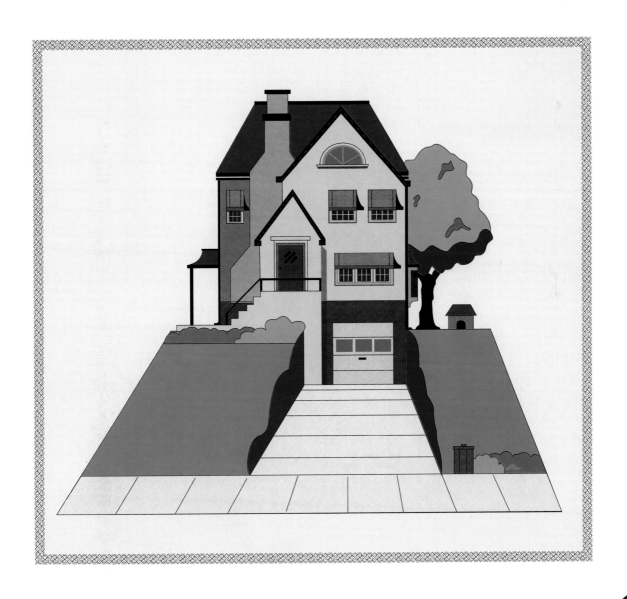

TASK 46

Inserting a Graphic

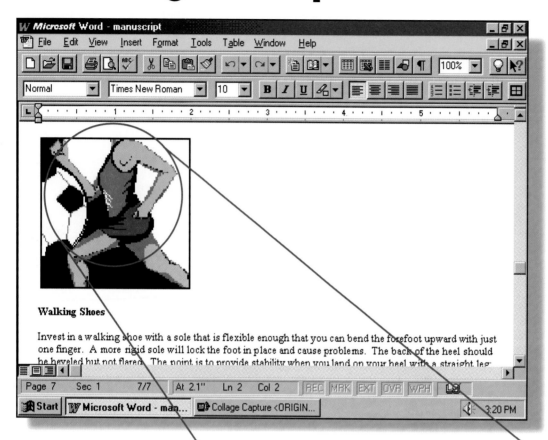

"Why would I do this?"

Word for Windows lets you insert pictures in your document in order to add emphasis and visual impact. Graphics can liven up any document. For example, if you were typing a newsletter article about walking shoes, you could insert a sports graphic below the article.

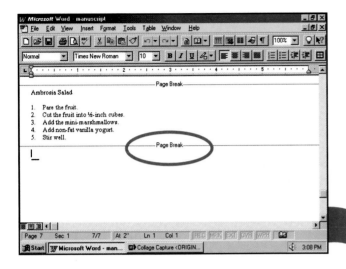

1 Press **Ctrl+End** or scroll to the bottom of the document. Then press **Ctrl+Enter** to insert a page break.

2 On page 7, type the text that appears in the figure so that your computer screen matches the screen shown here.

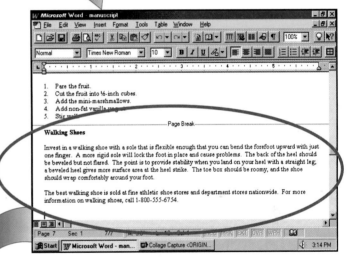

3 Click **Insert** in the menu bar, and then click **Picture**. Word opens the Insert Picture dialog box. Click the **Up One Level** button on the Insert Picture toolbar. Then double-click the CLIPART folder. The files in the CLIPART folder are displayed. Word for Windows comes with several clip-art images you can insert in your document.

4 In the files list, click **Sports**. This selects the graphic you want to insert. Click the **Preview** button on the Insert Picture toolbar to preview the graphic on the right side of the dialog box.

5 Click **OK**. The graphic appears on-screen in the default position and size. You can change the box's position and size.

6 Click the graphic. This selects the graphic so you can move it. Selection handles appear along the sides of the picture. Handles are the solid boxes at the corners and sides of the frame.

WHY WORRY?

To delete the graphic, click the graphic to select it, and then press Delete.

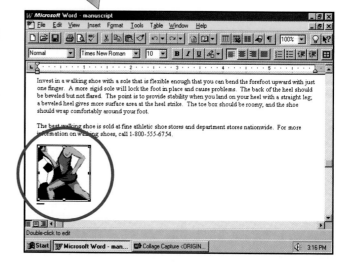

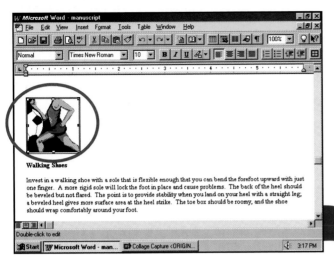

7 Click and hold down the mouse button and drag the graphic above the heading. Release the mouse button.

8 To resize the graphic, move the mouse pointer to the top middle selection handle. When the mouse pointer changes to a double-headed arrow, drag the graphic up about 1/2 inch. This makes a graphic taller.

WHY WORRY?

Follow the same procedures to move the picture back to its original location or to change the picture back to its original size.

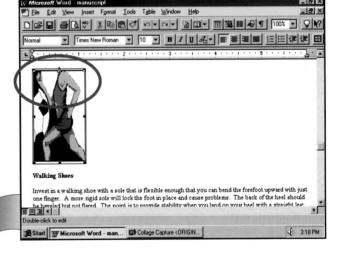

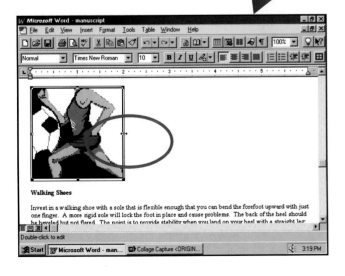

9 Move the mouse pointer to the right-middle selection handle, and when the mouse pointer changes to a double-headed arrow, drag the graphic to the right about one inch. This makes the graphic wider. Click outside the graphic to deselect it. ∎

Creating a Table

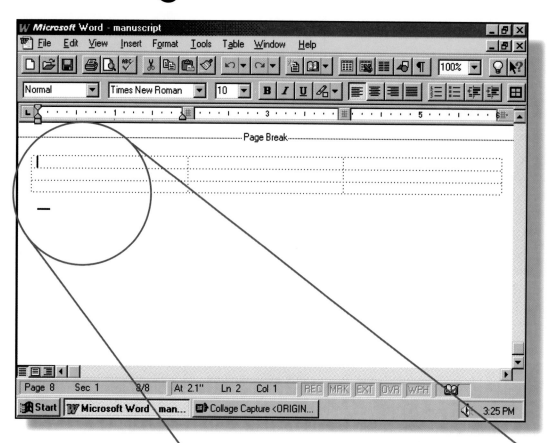

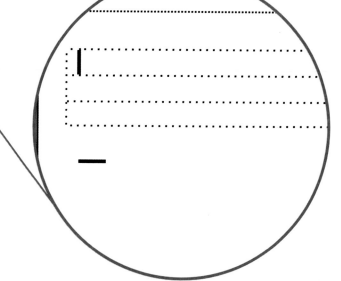

"Why would I do this?"

Tables are easier to work with than tabs are if you have to set up a grid of information (columns and rows). You can organize items by columns and rows without calculating tab settings. A table looks similar to a worksheet in a spreadsheet program. You might want to create a table for an annual report or a sales report.

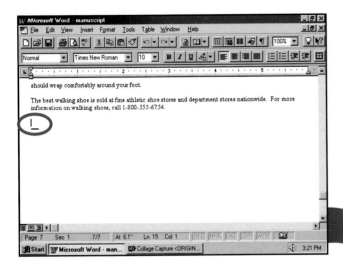

1 Press **Ctrl+End**. This moves the insertion point to the bottom of the document.

2 Press **Ctrl+Enter** to insert a page break. Then scroll down so that only page 8 shows on-screen.

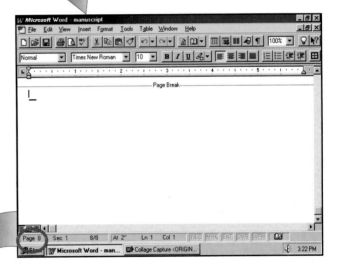

3 Click the **Insert Table** button on the Standard toolbar. Word for Windows displays a grid below the Insert Table button.

4 Hold down the left mouse button and drag over the grid to highlight three columns and three rows. You see `3 x 3 Table` at the bottom of the grid. This tells Word for Windows to create a three-column table with three rows.

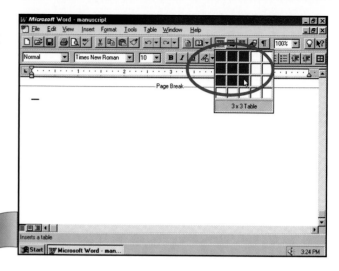

NOTE ▼

You can always add or delete rows later, so don't worry about getting them right.

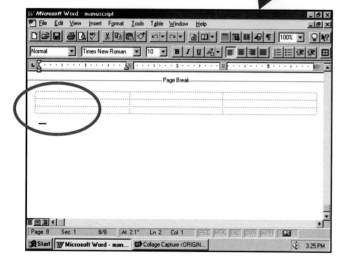

5 When you release the mouse button, Word inserts a table with three columns and three rows on-screen. ■

NOTE ▼

You can convert text into a table by using tabs to separate columns and paragraph marks to indicate the end of rows. Then select the text and choose Table, Convert Text to Table and select the options you want.

WHY WORRY?

To delete the table, click the Undo button on the Standard toolbar immediately.

Entering Text in a Table

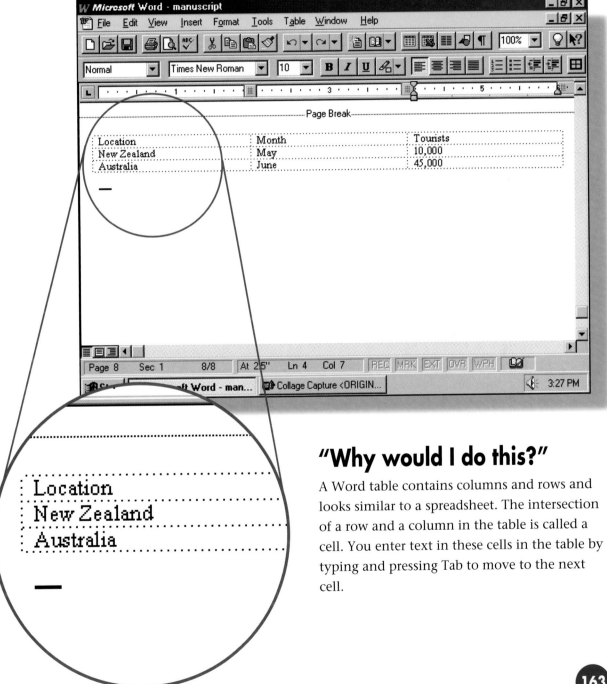

"Why would I do this?"

A Word table contains columns and rows and looks similar to a spreadsheet. The intersection of a row and a column in the table is called a cell. You enter text in these cells in the table by typing and pressing Tab to move to the next cell.

1 Type **Location** and press **Tab**. This enters information into the first cell in the table and moves the insertion point to the next column in that row.

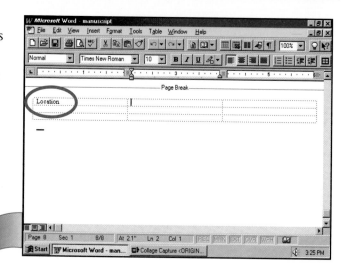

2 Type **Month** and press **Tab** to enter information in that cell and move the insertion point to the next column.

NOTE ▼

Pressing Shift+Tab will move you back to the previous cell.

3 Type **Tourists**. This completes the headings for the table.

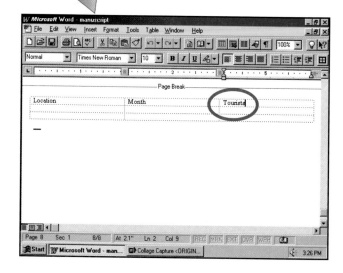

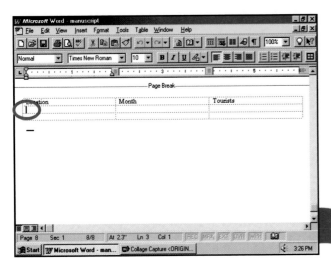

4 Press **Tab** to move the insertion point to the first cell in the next row.

5 Type **New Zealand** and press **Tab**. Type **May** and press **Tab**. Type **10,000** and press **Tab**. This enters the text for the first row and moves the insertion point to the next row.

> **NOTE** ▼
>
> You can convert a table to text by selecting the table and choosing Table, Convert Table to Text. Then choose the character you want to use to separate the columns.

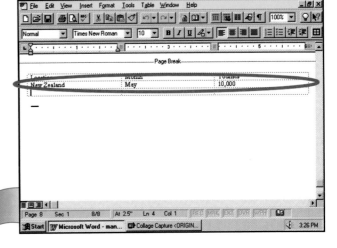

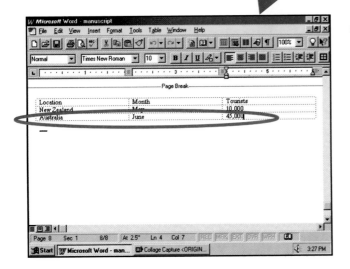

6 Type **Australia** and press **Tab**. Type **June** and press **Tab**. Type **45,000**. This completes the text for the table. ■

> **WHY WORRY?**
>
> Make corrections in the table as you would in a normal document. You press Enter within a cell to insert a line break.

Adding a Row and Deleting a Row in a Table

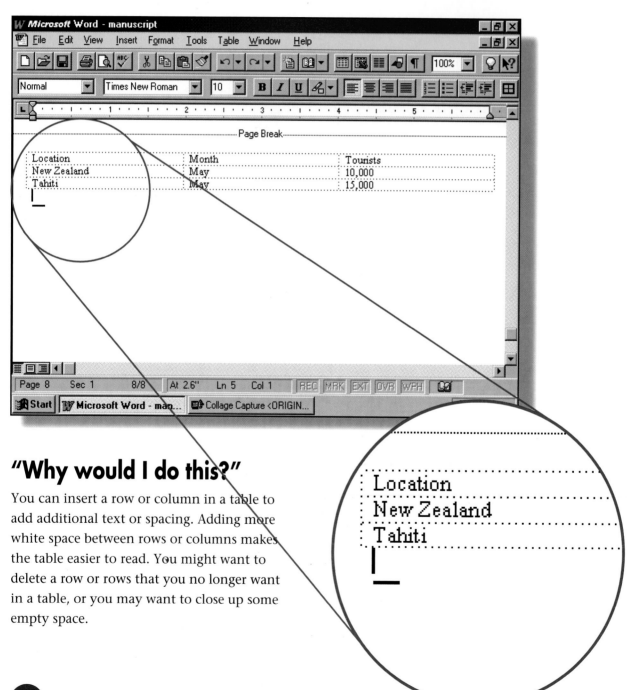

"Why would I do this?"

You can insert a row or column in a table to add additional text or spacing. Adding more white space between rows or columns makes the table easier to read. You might want to delete a row or rows that you no longer want in a table, or you may want to close up some empty space.

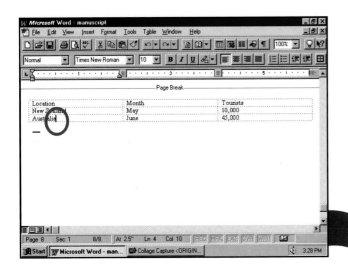

1 Put the insertion point where you want to insert a row. To access the Table commands, you have to put the insertion point within the table first.

2 Open the **Table** menu and click **Insert Rows**. A row is inserted in the table.

> **NOTE** ▼
>
> As a shortcut, you can put the insertion point in the cell of the last row and column of the table and press Tab to create a new row.

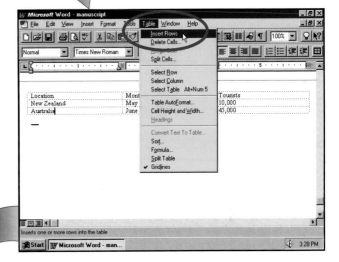

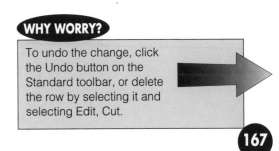

3 Click in the first cell of the new row. Then type **Tahiti** and press **Tab**. Type **May** and press **Tab**. Type **15,000**. This enters the text for the new row.

> **WHY WORRY?**
>
> To undo the change, click the Undo button on the Standard toolbar, or delete the row by selecting it and selecting Edit, Cut.

4 To delete a row, put the insertion point in the row you want to delete. Drag across the entire row.

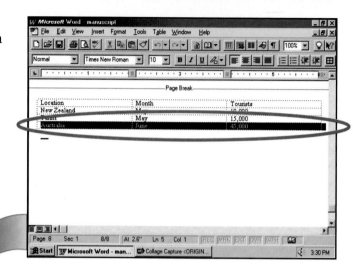

5 Click **Table** in the menu bar. Then click **Delete Cells**. You see the Delete Cells dialog box. Click **Delete Entire Row** and click **OK**.

NOTE ▼

To quickly delete a row, click in the left margin of the row you want to delete. Then choose Table, Delete Rows.

6 The row is deleted. ■

WHY WORRY?

To undo the change, click the Undo button on the Standard toolbar.

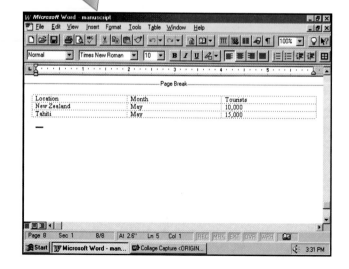

TASK 50

Creating a Two-Column Document

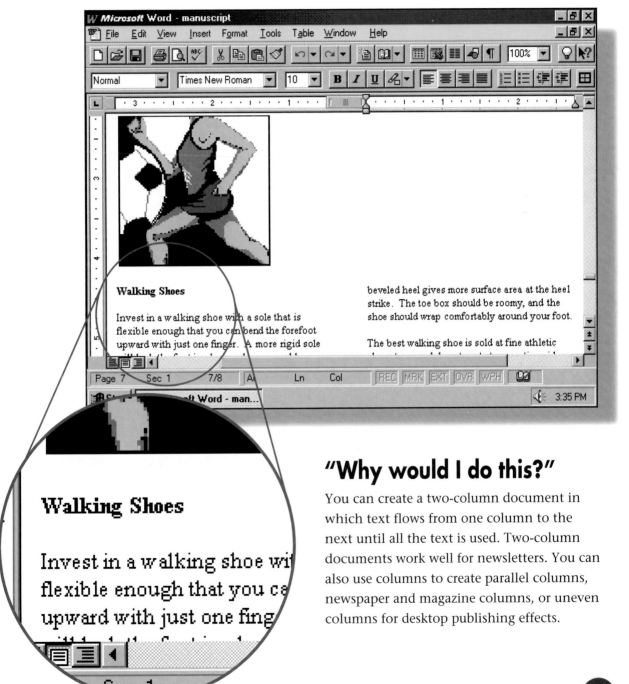

"Why would I do this?"

You can create a two-column document in which text flows from one column to the next until all the text is used. Two-column documents work well for newsletters. You can also use columns to create parallel columns, newspaper and magazine columns, or uneven columns for desktop publishing effects.

1 Move the insertion point to page 7. Select all the text, including the title. This tells Word for Windows where you want to create the columns.

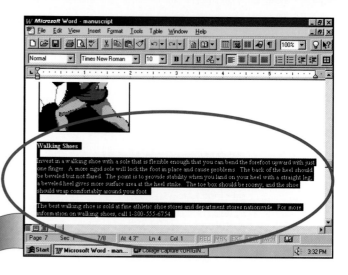

2 Click the **Columns** button on the Standard toolbar. Word for Windows displays a four-column toolbar below the Columns button.

3 Hold down the left mouse button and drag over the columns to highlight two columns. You see 2 Columns at the bottom of the columns. This tells Word for Windows to create two columns.

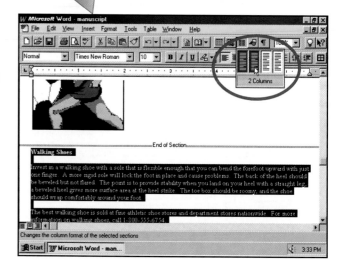

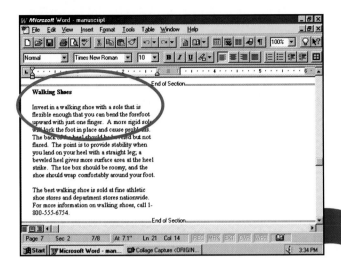

4 Release the mouse button. Then click anywhere to deselect the text. On-screen, you cannot see the two columns. To do so, you must switch to Page Layout view.

5 Click the **Page Layout View** button. You now have a two-column page. The current text is reformatted into two columns. ■

WHY WORRY?

To undo the columns, click the Undo button on the Standard toolbar immediately. You also can select the text in the columns, click the Columns button on the Standard toolbar, and highlight one column.

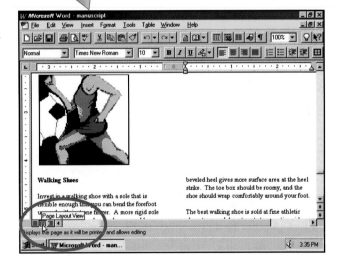

Inserting a WordArt Object

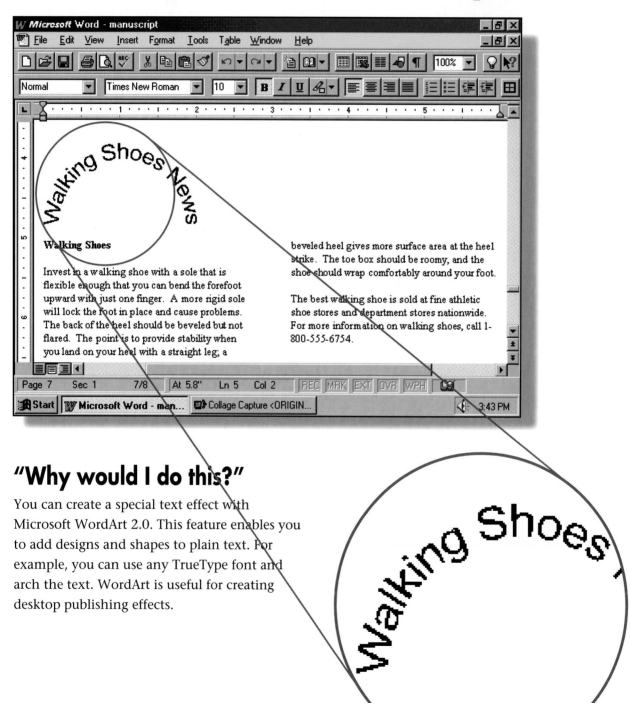

"Why would I do this?"

You can create a special text effect with Microsoft WordArt 2.0. This feature enables you to add designs and shapes to plain text. For example, you can use any TrueType font and arch the text. WordArt is useful for creating desktop publishing effects.

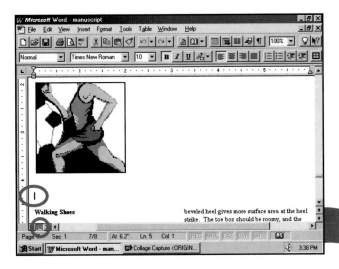

1 Click the **Page Layout View** button on the status bar. Click above *Walking Shoes*. Press **Enter** three times to insert three blank lines. Then press the up arrow key to move the insertion point up one line to where you want to insert the object.

2 Click **Insert** in the menu bar. Then click **Object**. You see the Object dialog box. The Create New tab is selected. Double-click **Microsoft WordArt 2.0**. This tells Word for Windows that you want to insert a WordArt object. You may have to scroll through the list to find this option.

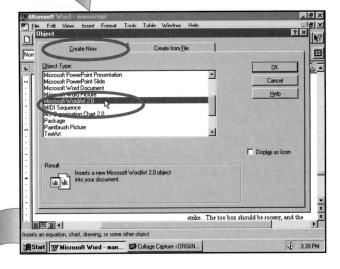

3 In the Enter Your Text Here dialog box, type **Walking Shoes News**.

4 Click the down arrow next to the Plain Text option on the WordArt Toolbar. Then click the arch in the third row, first column. This tells Word for Windows you want to arch the text.

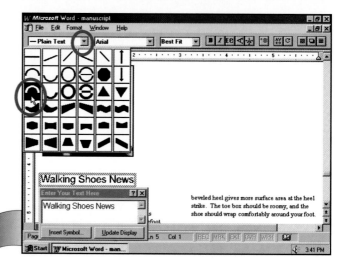

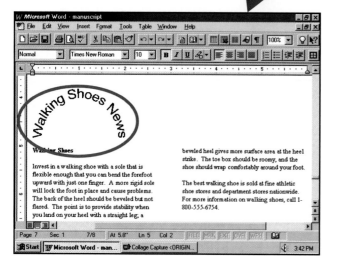

5 Click in the document. Then click outside the selected object. This inserts the object in the document and returns you to the document. ■

WHY WORRY?

To edit the object, double-click it. To delete the object, click once on it and press Delete.

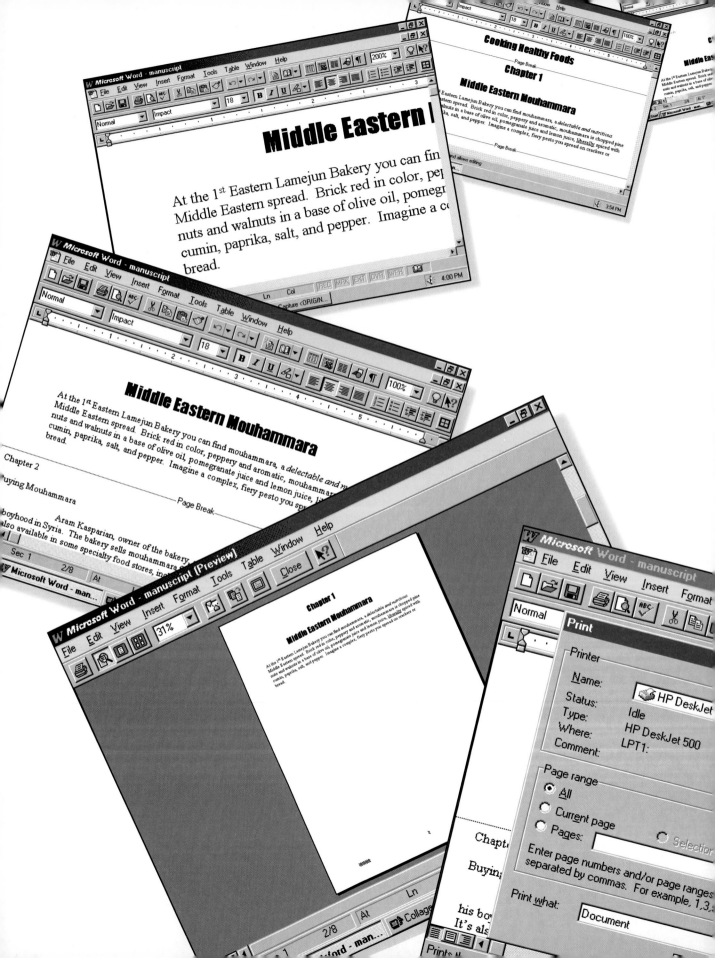

PART VIII

Viewing and Printing the Document

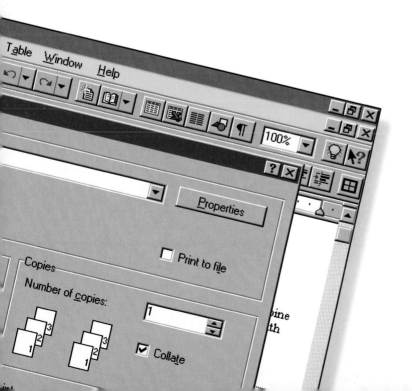

n this part, you learn how to change the view of your document, preview your document, and then print your document.

Word provides three views for your document: Normal, Outline, and Page Layout. Normal is the standard editing view you've been using. Outline view helps you create outlines. Page Layout view enables you to display multiple columns, headers and footers, and footnotes as they will be printed.

Word's Zoom feature works with any view. It lets you enlarge or reduce the view of a page on-screen. You can make text on the screen appear smaller or larger; it may show the whole page or a smaller section of it at higher magnification.

Print Preview is a view, but it's separate from the other views. With Word's Print Preview feature, you can review the appearance of the printed document before you produce the final output. (You can't edit in Print Preview.) The first page of the document appears in Print Preview as a reduced image in the Print Preview screen. You can use the Zoom feature in Print Preview to magnify the view. See your Microsoft Word documentation for complete information on Print Preview.

In Word, you can print your documents using a basic printing procedure, or you can enhance the printout using several page setup options (as explained in Part IV). The Print dialog box lets you print some or all the pages within a document, the current page, a range of pages, selected text, or multiple copies of the printout.

The first time you use your printer with Word, it is a good idea to check the Setup options. Word can use the options and capabilities that are available with each printer. Often, you will need to provide more details about your printer so that Word knows its capabilities. If you want to specify details about your printer, choose the File Print command and click the Printer button. Then you can confirm that you installed the right printer and connected it correctly, or you can switch to a different printer.

It is a good idea to save your documents before printing—just in case a printer error or other problem occurs. Therefore, you won't lose the work.

In this part, you learn how to print your document from the Print dialog box. But, if you have already set up your print options and you're back to the document, you can just click the Print button on the Standard toolbar to print your document.

This part introduces you to the basics of printing the document. With some experimentation and practice, you will be able to create some very interesting print results.

Displaying a Document in Page Layout View

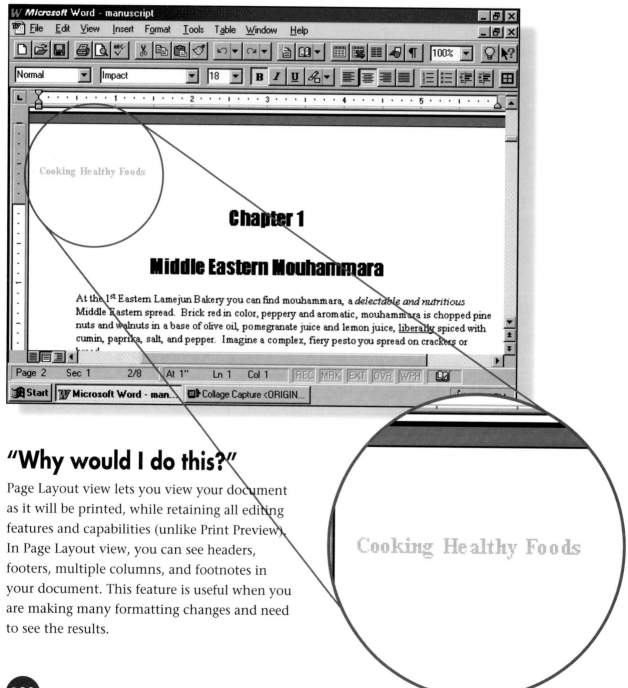

"Why would I do this?"

Page Layout view lets you view your document as it will be printed, while retaining all editing features and capabilities (unlike Print Preview). In Page Layout view, you can see headers, footers, multiple columns, and footnotes in your document. This feature is useful when you are making many formatting changes and need to see the results.

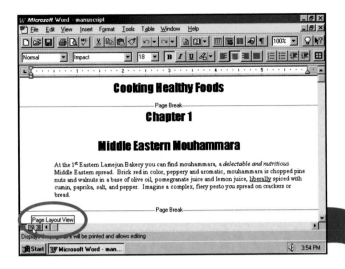

1 Click the **Page Layout View** button on the status bar (the button with a piece of paper and several horizontal lines). This selects the View Page Layout command.

2 You see the document in Page Layout view. As you can see, the header appears very light in this view.

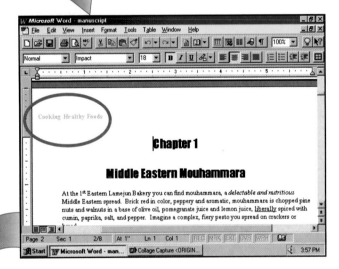

3 Click the **Normal View** button at the left end of the status bar (the button with several horizontal lines). This returns the document to normal view. ■

WHY WORRY?

The Page Layout command is not a toggle. To turn off Page Layout view, you must select another view. To return to Normal view, click the Normal View button on the status bar.

TASK 53

Zooming a Document

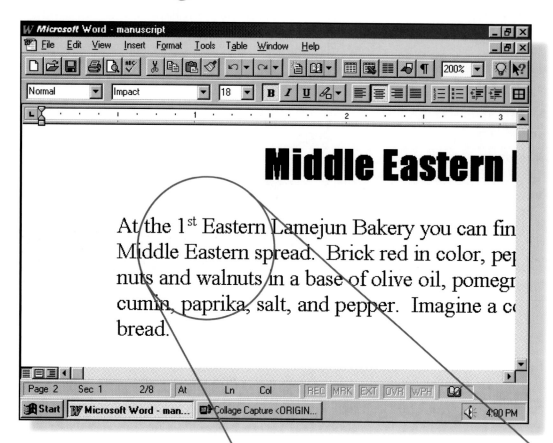

"Why would I do this?"

If you want to zoom in and get a closer look at text in your document, you select a higher percentage of magnification. For instance, if you work with small font sizes, you can inspect your text more closely without having to preview or print the worksheet. If you want to zoom out so the whole page shows on the screen at one glance, you select a lower percentage of magnification.

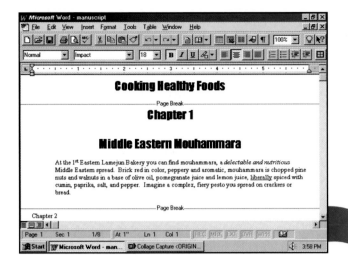

1 Press **Ctrl+Home** to go to the beginning of the document, if necessary.

2 Place the mouse pointer on the Zoom Control box on the Standard toolbar (the box with 100%).

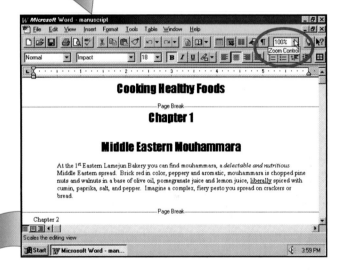

3 Click the down arrow next to the Zoom Control box on the Standard toolbar. The magnification percentages appear in the Zoom Control list.

4 Click **200%**. This enlarges the document to a magnification of 200 percent. Use the scroll bars to see more of the text in the document.

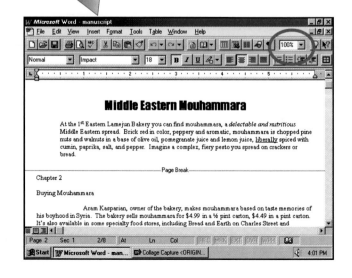

5 Click the down arrow next to the Zoom Control box again. Then click **50%**. This reduces the document to 50 percent and gives you a look at the overall picture.

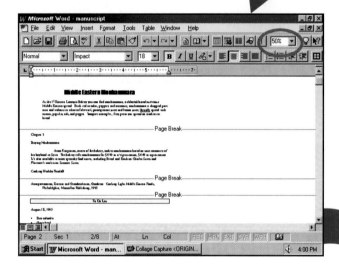

6 Click **100%** in the Zoom Control box to restore the document to 100 percent. ■

Previewing the Document

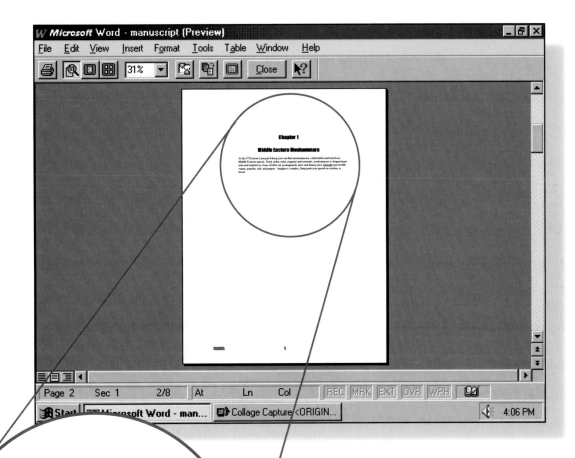

Chapter 1

Middle Eastern Mouhammara

At the 1ˢᵗ Eastern Lamejun Bakery you can find mouhammara, a *delectable and nutritious* Middle Eastern spread. Brick red in color, peppery and aromatic, mouhammara is chopped pine nuts and walnuts in a base of olive oil, pomegranate juice and lemon juice, liberally spiced with cumin, paprika, salt, and pepper. Imagine a complex, fiery pesto you spread on crackers or bread.

"Why would I do this?"

The Print Preview command lets you see document pages on-screen as they will appear printed on paper, including page numbers, headers, footers, fonts, fonts sizes and styles, orientation, and margins. Previewing your document is a great way to catch formatting errors, such as incorrect margins, overlapped text, boldfaced text, and other text enhancements. You will save costly printer paper and time by previewing your document before you print.

1 Click the **Print Preview** button on the Standard toolbar (the button with the piece of paper and a magnifying glass). Clicking the Print Preview button selects the Print Preview command.

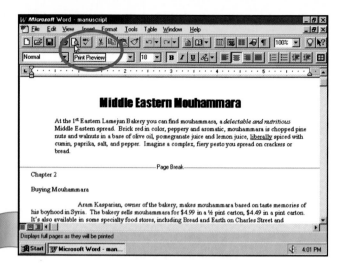

2 You see a preview of how your document will look when you print it. Click the **Next Page** button (double down arrow) at the bottom of the scroll bar to see the next page of your document.

3 Select the text at the top of page 2. The mouse pointer (usually an arrow) changes to a magnifying glass and a plus sign (+). This mouse pointer lets you magnify any portion of the page.

NOTE ▼

The Zoom Control box on the Print Preview toolbar lets you specify how large or small a document appears on the screen. Initially, it's 31 percent.

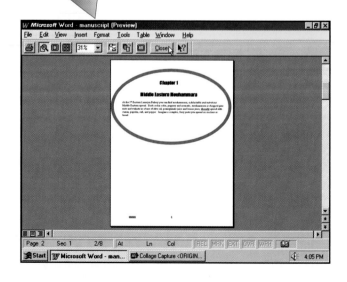

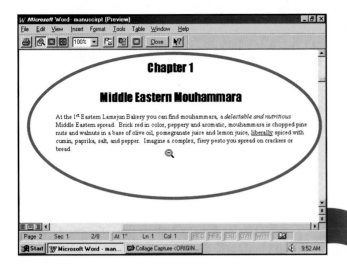

4 Click the selected text again. This zooms in on the top portion of your page and magnifies the text at 100 percent (as shown in the Zoom Control box). Notice the mouse pointer is a magnifying glass and a minus sign (–). This mouse pointer lets you zoom out and shrink the text on the page.

5 Click the text one more time. The text is restored to 31 percent magnification. To exit Print Preview, click the **Close (X)** button. This returns you to the document. ■

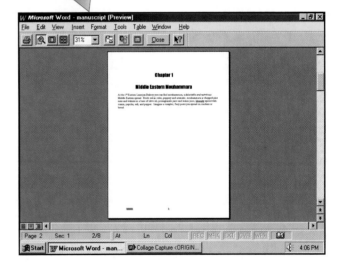

TASK 55
Printing the Document

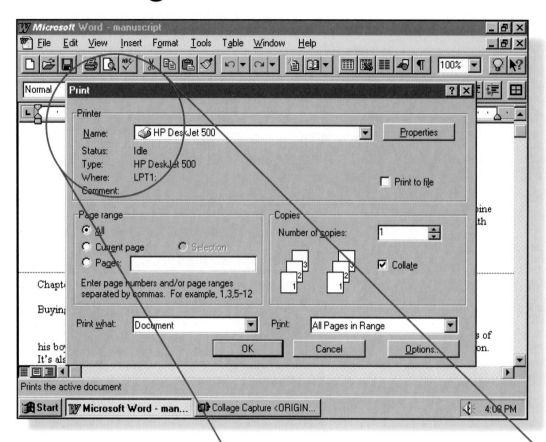

"Why would I do this?"

Word makes it easy to print a document and allows you to select the printer and font settings. You can print a single page, page ranges, or disconnected pages, as well as selected text. You also can specify the number of copies and collate the copies as you print. You might print a document that you need to give to others or that you need to file for reference.

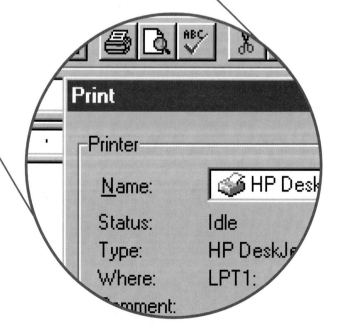

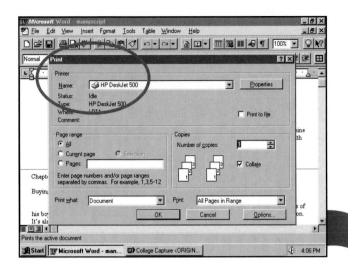

1 Click **File** in the menu bar and click **Print**. Word opens the Print dialog box. This dialog box controls which printer is used, what you print (the entire document, a range of pages, and so on), how many copies you print, and other options.

NOTE ▼

You can also press Ctrl+P to select the File Print command.

2 Choose any printing options you want. The Pages option is selected in the figure, and 1–3 appears in the Pages text box. This tells Word to print pages 1 through 3.

NOTE ▼

To print disconnected pages, enter a comma between the page numbers and page ranges. For example, you could type 1,3,7,9-15,20.

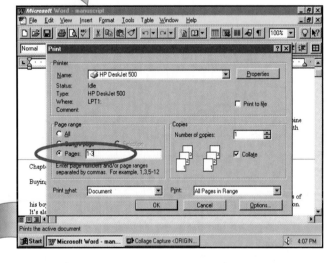

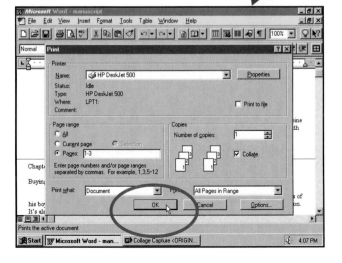

3 Click **OK** to start printing the document. ▪

WHY WORRY?

While the document is printing, Word displays a dialog box on-screen. To stop the print job, click Cancel.

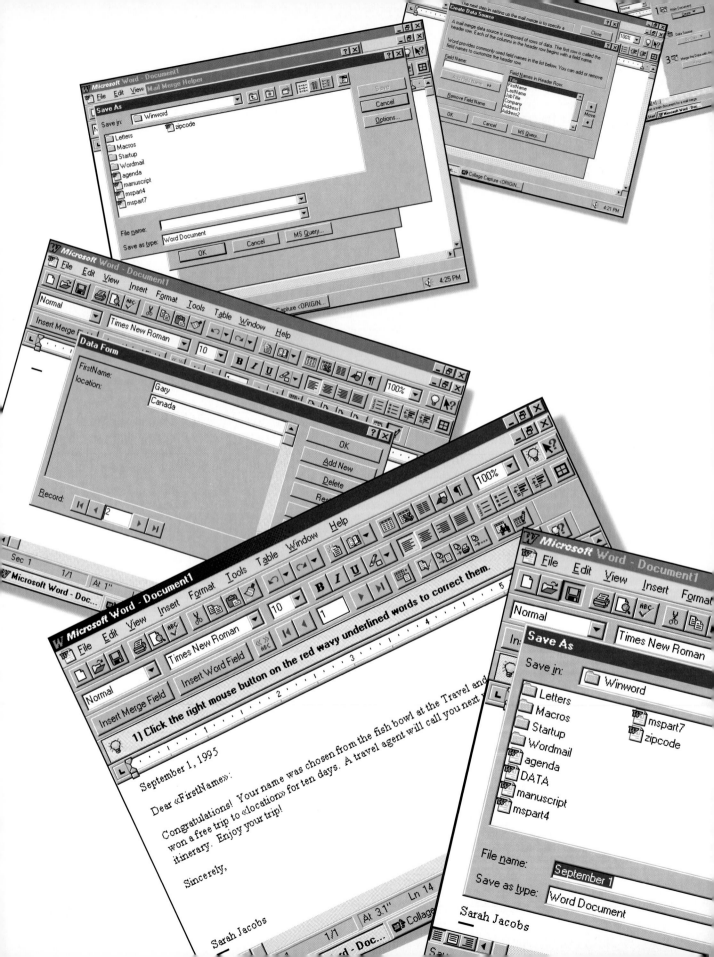

PART IX

Merging Documents

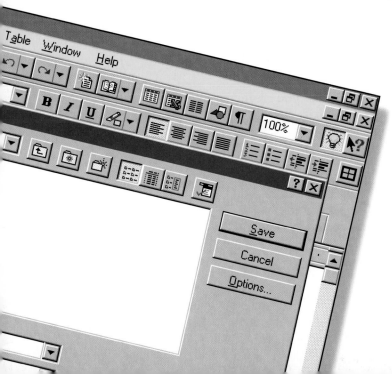

I n this part, you learn how to create a merge letter—a fairly complex process. However, it is easier than it looks. The tasks in this part build on each other. Therefore, it is important that you follow all the tasks in the section to complete the merge process.

Two files make up a basic merge procedure: the data source and the main document. The main document contains the unchanging text and the codes that control the merge. The data source contains the variable information you want inserted into the main document.

There are several tasks you must follow to create a merge letter. First, you create the main document. Next, you create the data source. Word provides several predefined fields to use in the data source, or you can create your own. If you have created a contact list in Schedule+ (another component in the Microsoft Office suite) or a personal address book in the Microsoft Exchange (a component of Windows 95), you can use these records as a data source.

After saving the data source, you're ready to enter records. A record is one set of information, such as all the information about one person. Each individual element in the record, such as the first name, the last name, or the phone number, is stored in a field. You will create a document for each record you enter, and it will contain the specific information in that record.

Next, you type the main document. The main document contains the letter's text—the information you want each letter to contain. The main document also includes the codes that control the merge. You need to know the names of the fields you created in the data source so that you can insert the right code into the main document.

After you create the main document, you save the file. The final step is to merge the two files. A new file will be created that contains a letter for each record in the data source. You can either save or print the new file.

Word's Mail Merge feature offers many options that you may want to experiment with on your own. This book provides only the simplest of examples. If you want more information, see your Microsoft Word documentation.

This part also shows you how to create envelopes and labels. Word gives you two ways to print addresses on envelopes or labels. If you want to print addresses on envelopes or labels individually, use the Tools, Envelopes and Labels command. Word will print the return address and the mailing address on the envelope or label. If you want to print many envelopes or labels at one time, you can use the Merge feature to do a mass mailing.

Creating a Main Document

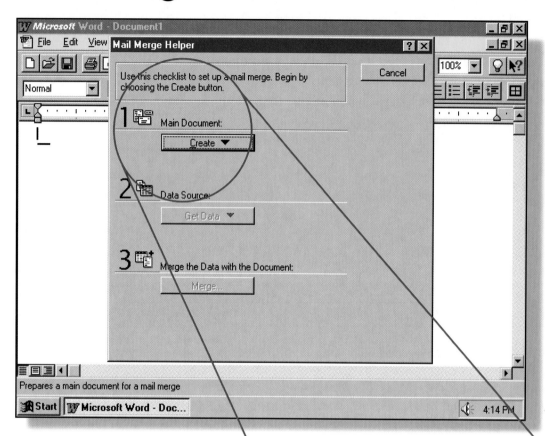

"Why would I do this?"

Instead of typing many individual letters and changing the variable information in each letter, you can tell Word to merge the letter and the variable information, which saves you typing and time. Before you can merge files, you must create a main document file. The main document file contains field names (such as {Name} and {Address}) and the information that remains constant (such as the body of the letter and your signature line). Your main document might be an invitation, a product announcement, or a price list.

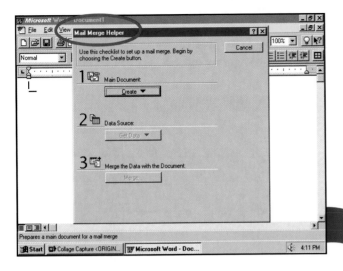

1 Click **Tools** on the menu bar. Then click **Mail Merge**. Word opens the Merge Mail Helper dialog box. Select the type of file you want to create.

2 Click **Create** to display a drop-down list of options from which you choose the type of main document you are creating. Click **Form Letters**. Word asks whether you want to open a new document or create the document within the active window.

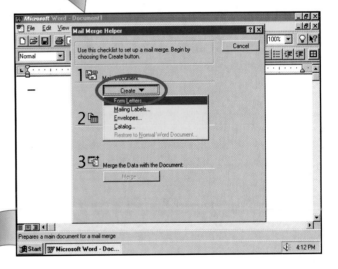

3 Click **Active Window**. If the active window contains an exciting document, choose New Main Document. You are returned to the Mail Merge Helper dialog box. Next you create the data source, as explained in Task 57. ∎

WHY WORRY?

If you don't want to create the main document, click Cancel.

195

Creating a Data Source

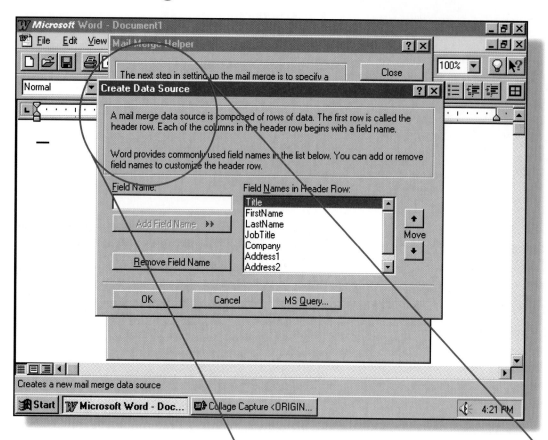

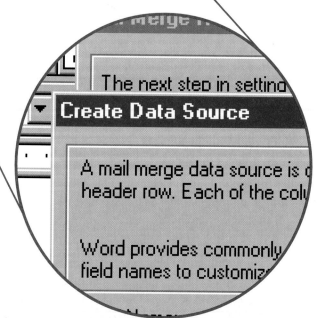

"Why would I do this?"

The data source stores the variable information that you want to insert into the form field. Each piece of information is stored in a field (such as {First Name}). A complete set of information (such as all the information about John Smith) is called a record. Perhaps you want to create a data source file of addresses for batch mailing.

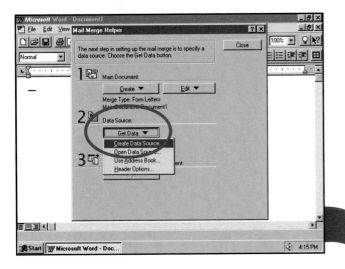

1 From the Mail Merge Helper dialog box, click **Get Data**. Word displays a drop-down list of data source options. Click **Create Data Source**.

NOTE ▼

To use addresses from Microsoft Schedule+ or the Microsoft Exchange, choose Use Address Book from the Get Data menu. Then choose Schedule+ Contact List or Personal Address Book and follow the instructions as prompted.

2 You see the Create Data Source dialog box. This box includes a field name list with common field names. Instead of trying to figure out all the fields you'll need, you can eliminate the default fields you don't want. Also, you can add new field names.

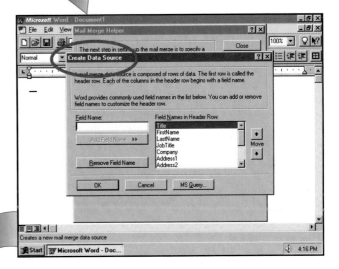

3 Type **Location**. This enters a new field name in the Field Name text box.

4 Click **Add Field Name**, and Word adds this field to the bottom of the list for your data source.

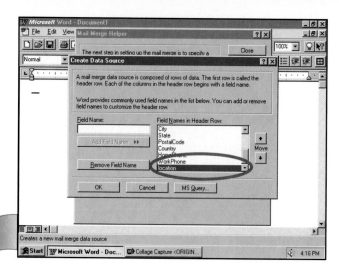

5 In the Field Names in Header Row list, scroll to the top of the list and click **Title**. This selects a field you don't need.

6 Click **Remove Field Name** to remove the field.

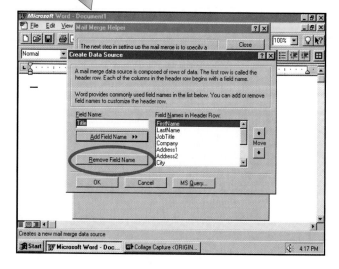

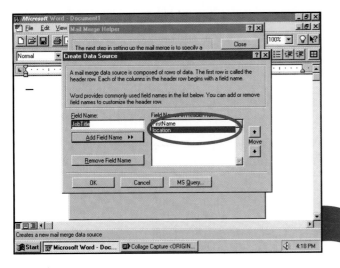

7 Follow steps 5 and 6 to remove these predefined fields: LastName, JobTitle, Company, Address1, Address2, City, State, PostalCode, Country, HomePhone, and WorkPhone. Now you have only the two fields you need: FirstName and Location.

8 Click **OK** to complete the Field Name list.

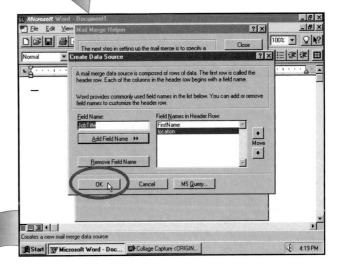

9 The Save As dialog box is displayed so that you can save the field. See the next task. ■

WHY WORRY?

If you don't want to save the data source, click Cancel.

Saving the Data Source

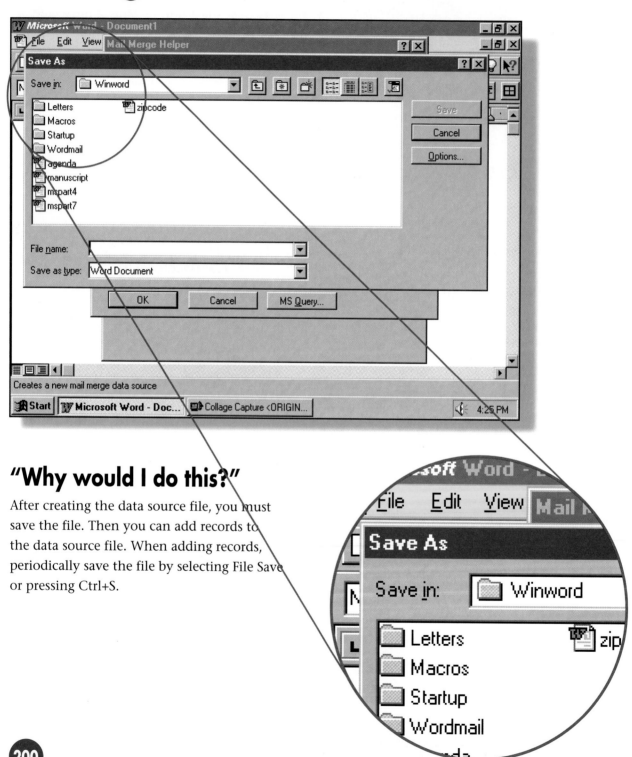

"Why would I do this?"

After creating the data source file, you must save the file. Then you can add records to the data source file. When adding records, periodically save the file by selecting File Save or pressing Ctrl+S.

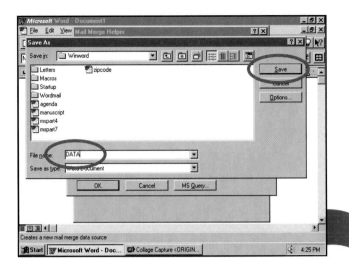

1 After you enter the field names, type **DATA** in the File name text box of the Save As dialog box. The current folder in the figure is Winword; that is where the file will be saved. This enters the name for the data source. Click **Save** to save the document.

2 You are reminded that no records have been created. Click **Edit Data Source** to tell Word that you will add the records.

WHY WORRY?

If you don't want to save the file, click Cancel.

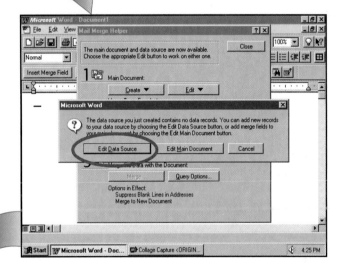

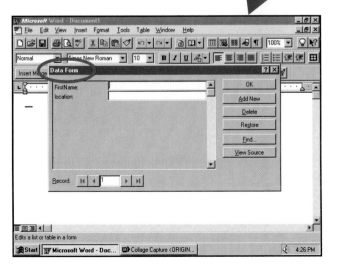

3 You see the Data Form dialog box. To complete this box, proceed to the next task. ∎

TASK 59

Entering Records into the Data Source

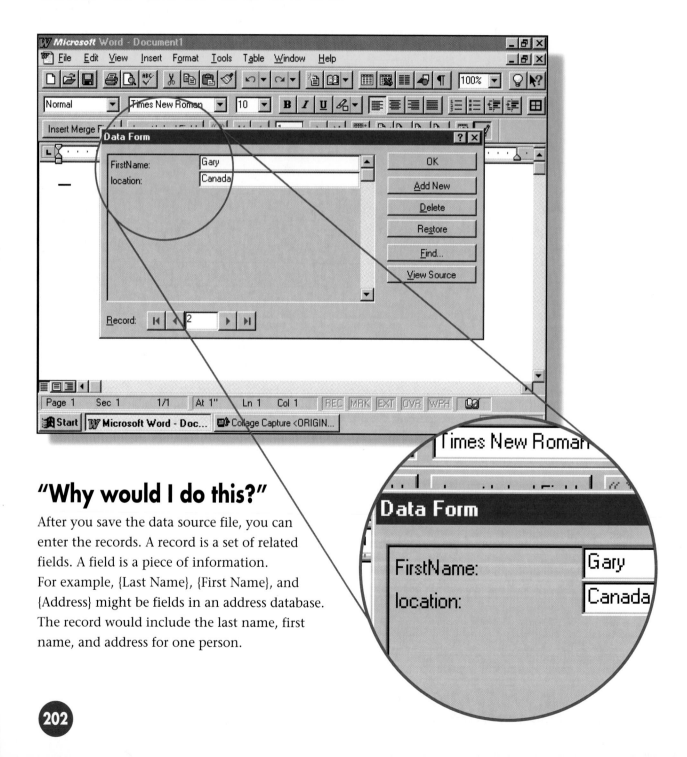

"Why would I do this?"

After you save the data source file, you can enter the records. A record is a set of related fields. A field is a piece of information. For example, {Last Name}, {First Name}, and {Address} might be fields in an address database. The record would include the last name, first name, and address for one person.

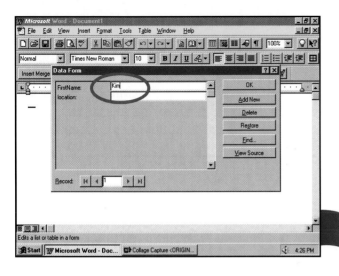

1 After you save the data source, type **Kim** in the FirstName text box of the Data Form dialog box. This enters the information for the first field. When you merge the documents, this specific text will be inserted into the document.

2 Press **Tab** to move the insertion point to the Location text box. Then type **Europe**. This enters the specific location for this person. This information (the name and location) is stored in a record.

WHY WORRY?

If you make a mistake while typing, correct it as you would in any other document.

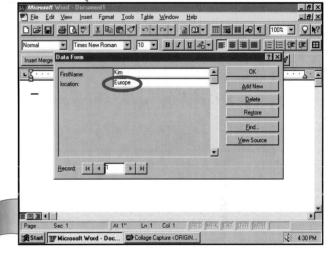

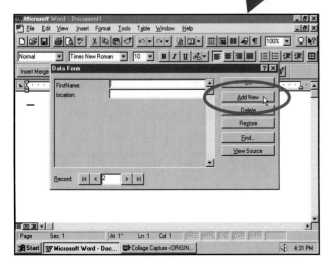

3 Click **Add New**. The current record is added to the document. The text boxes clear, and the record count is incremented by one. The next record can be entered.

4 Type **Gary**. This enters the information in the first field of the second record.

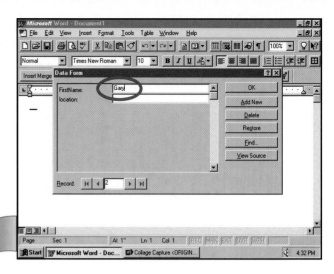

5 Press **Tab** to move the insertion point to the next field. Then type **Canada** to enter the information for the next field. Click **Add New Record** to add the record to your data document.

6 Click **OK**. This returns you to the main document. The Mail Merge toolbar is displayed. In the next task, you will type the main document. ■

NOTE ▼

To delete a record, use the Record scroll arrows at the bottom of the Data Form to display the record you want. Then click the Delete button.

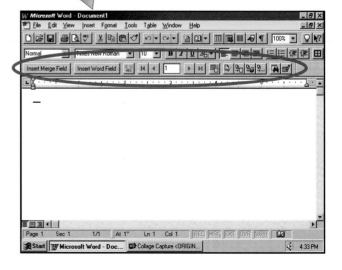

Typing the Main Document

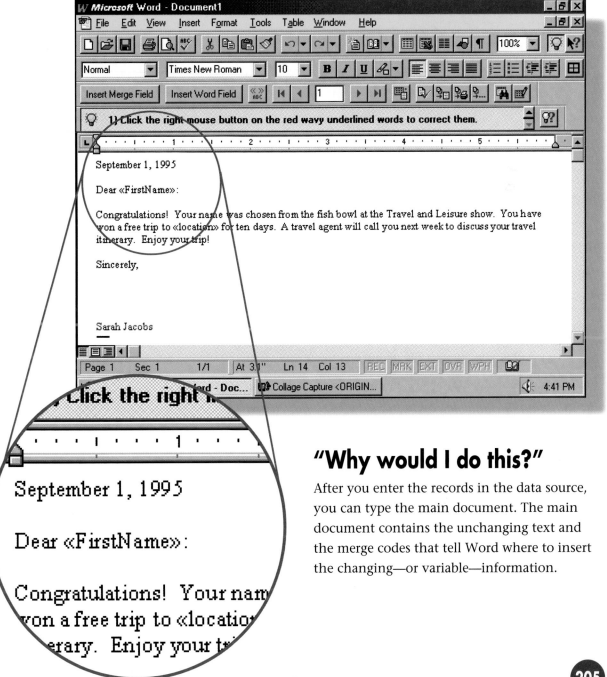

"Why would I do this?"

After you enter the records in the data source, you can type the main document. The main document contains the unchanging text and the merge codes that tell Word where to insert the changing—or variable—information.

205

1 Type **September 1, 1995** and press **Enter** twice. Type **Dear** and press the **Spacebar**. This enters the beginning text for the main document. Now you are ready to insert a field.

WHY WORRY?

If you make a mistake while typing, correct it as you would in any regular document.

2 Click **Insert Merge Field**. Word displays a drop-down list of field names.

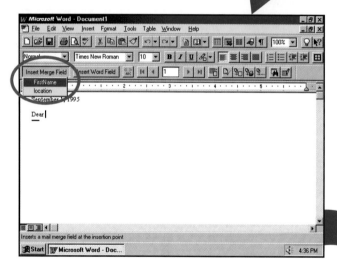

3 Click **FirstName**. This inserts the field name. You see the field code on-screen. This code tells Word to insert the information into the first field of each record.

WHY WORRY?

If you insert the field incorrectly, select it and press the Delete key. Then try again.

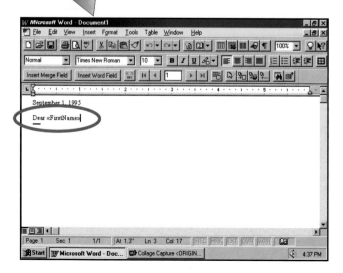

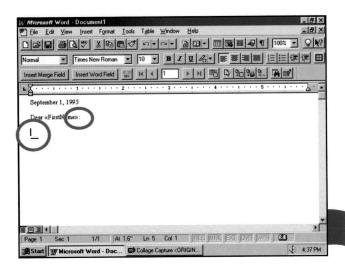

4 Type **:** and press **Enter** twice. The insertion point moves down two lines. This finishes the greeting for the letter.

5 Type the body of the letter: **Congratulations! Your name was chosen from the fish bowl at the Travel and Leisure show. You have won a free trip to**. This enters more of the unchanging text. Be sure to press the **Spacebar** after *to*. You are now ready to insert the next field.

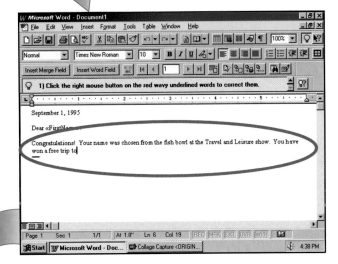

6 Click **Insert Merge Field**. Word displays a drop-down list of field names.

207

7 Click **Location** to insert the field code into your document. You will see the field code on-screen. This code tells Word to insert the information into the first field of each record.

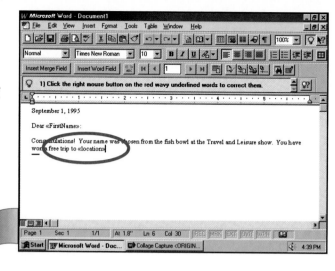

8 Type the rest of the letter: **for ten days. A travel agent will call you next week to discuss your travel itinerary. Enjoy your trip!**

9 Type the letter closing:

Sincerely,

Sarah Jacobs

This completes the letter. To save this completed letter, perform the steps as described in the next task. ■

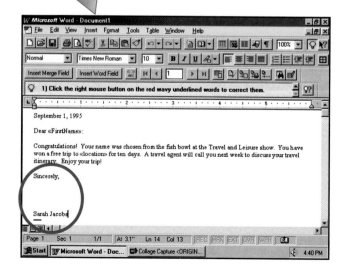

Saving the
Main Document

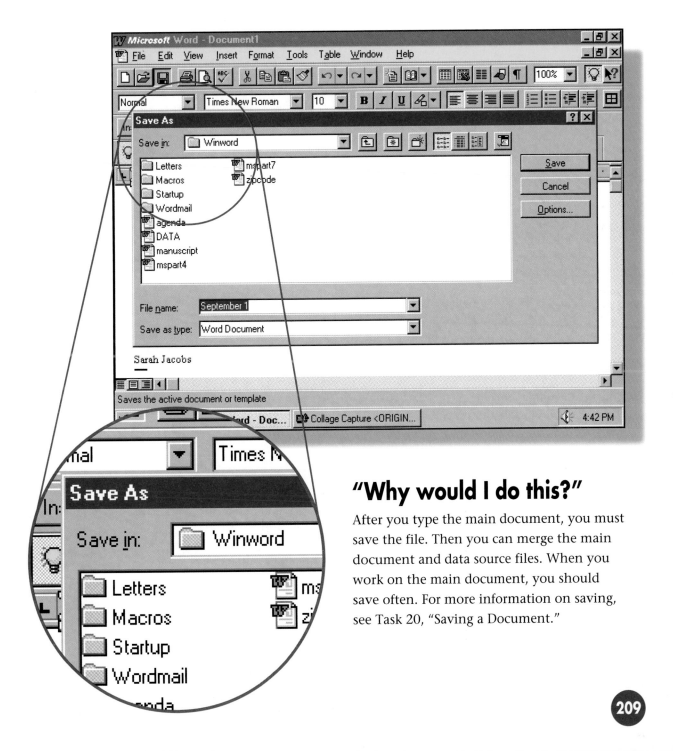

"Why would I do this?"

After you type the main document, you must
save the file. Then you can merge the main
document and data source files. When you
work on the main document, you should
save often. For more information on saving,
see Task 20, "Saving a Document."

1 Click **File** on the menu bar. Then click **Save As**. You see the Save As dialog box. September 1 appears in the File name text box; it's the default name that Word copied from the first line of your document.

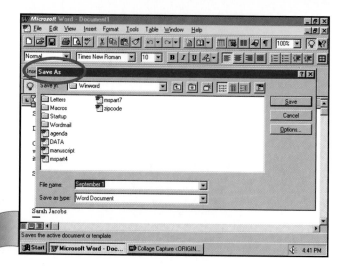

2 Type **MAIN**. This enters the name for the main document. The current folder in the figure is Winword. That is where the file will be saved. Click **Save** to save the document.

WHY WORRY?

If you don't want to save the file, click Cancel.

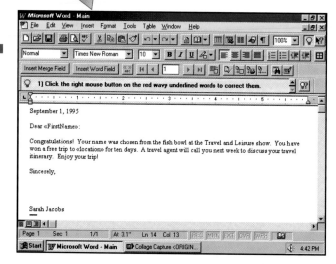

3 The document remains open on-screen, and the file name appears in the title bar. ■

Merging the Files

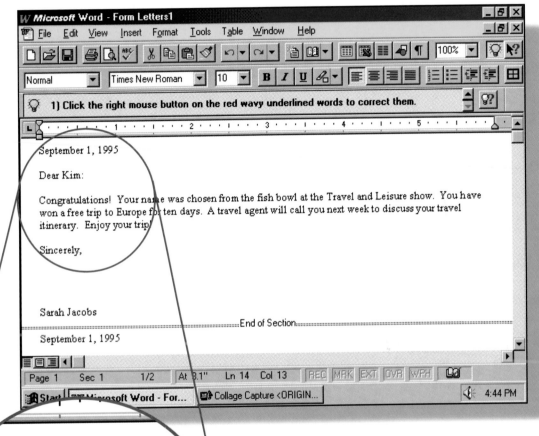

"Why would I do this?"

The last step in the merge process is to merge the main document file and the data source file. Word will create a new file that contains a letter for each record in the data source. You can save the new file or just print it. The Mail Merge feature offers many options that enable you to control how a merge is performed. For example, you can merge to the printer or merge all letters into a document with each letter on a separate page.

211

1 Click on Tools in the menu bar, and click **Mail Merge Helper**. You see the Mail Merge Helper dialog box. Click **Merge**.

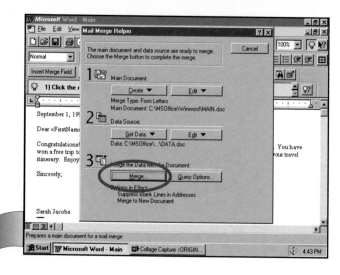

2 Word displays the Merge dialog box. Options here enable you to control which records are merged, where the letters are created, and other choices. For our example, the default options are acceptable. Click **Merge**.

3 A *custom* letter is created for each record in the data source file. The form letter's text is the same. For each field code, information is pulled from the data source. Scroll to page 2 to see the second merge letter. ■

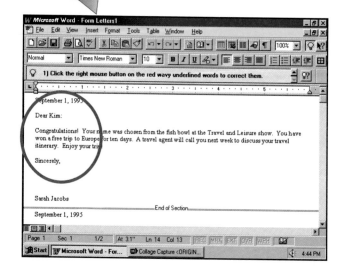

WHY WORRY?

If the merge didn't go as planned, check to make sure you set up each file correctly.

Creating Envelopes

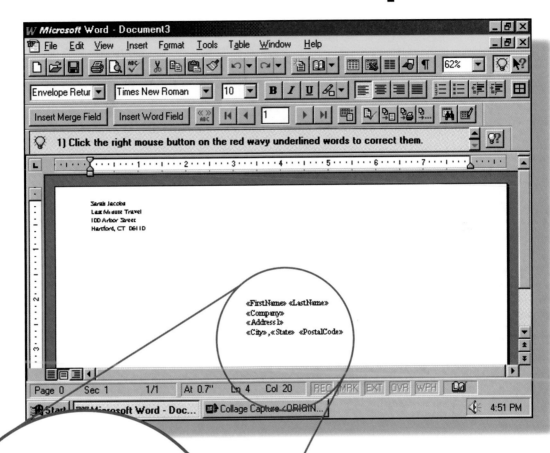

"Why would I do this?"

Word for Windows' Envelope feature lets you print addresses on envelopes. You can print the return address and then use the Mail Merge feature to print the mailing addresses on the envelopes. In order to use this feature, you must have a printer that can print on envelopes.

1 Open the **Tools** menu and choose **Mail Merge** to display the Mail Merge Helper dialog box. Click **Create** to display a drop-down list of options. Then click **Envelopes**. This tells Word that you are creating envelopes.

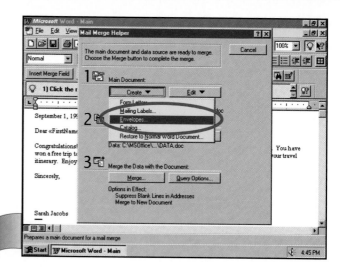

2 Word asks whether you want to change the document type or create a new main document. Click **New Main Document**. You are returned to the Mail Merge Helper dialog box to select a data source for merging.

3 In the Mail Merge Helper dialog box, click **Get Data**. Then click **Open Data Source**. You see the Open Data Source dialog box.

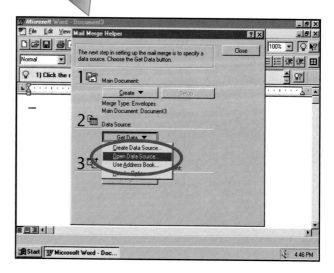

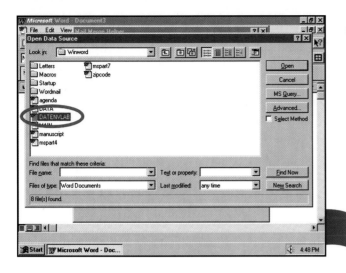

4 In the files and folders list, double-click the data source file you want to use. This tells Word to open the data file containing your address records.

5 Click **Set Up Main Document** to tell Word that you want to type in the main document.

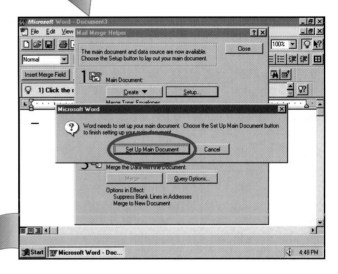

6 You see the Envelope Options dialog box. For our example, the default options are acceptable. Click **OK**.

215

7 The Envelope Address dialog box appears. This is where you insert merge codes that tell Word where to insert the information for the mailing address on the envelope. Click the **Insert Merge Field** button. Then choose a merge field. This figure shows the default merge fields for merging envelopes. Repeat this step for each merge field, as shown in the figure. When you finish, click **OK** and click **Close**.

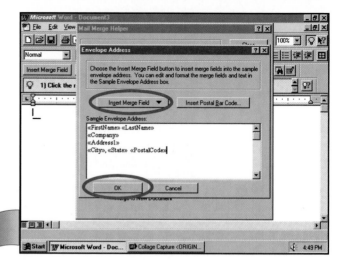

8 Type or edit the return address on the envelope form. (By default, your name appears in the Return address area.) Save the file and name it ENVELOPE. Then click the **Merge to Printer** button on the Mail Merge toolbar. You see the Print dialog box.

9 Insert an envelope in the printer or use an envelope tray to feed envelopes into your printer. Then click **OK** to start printing addresses on the envelopes. ■

WHY WORRY?

If the merge didn't go as planned, check that you set up each file correctly.

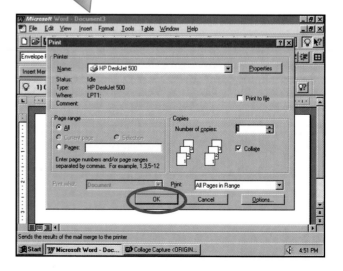

Creating Labels

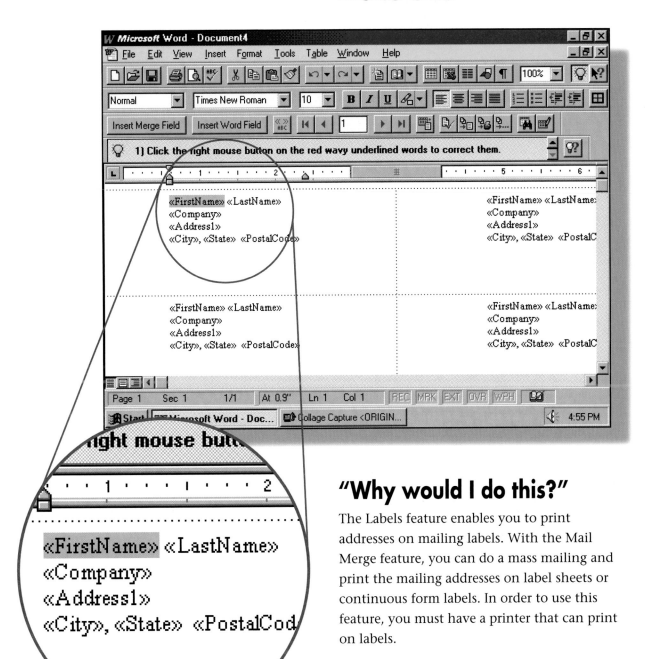

"Why would I do this?"

The Labels feature enables you to print addresses on mailing labels. With the Mail Merge feature, you can do a mass mailing and print the mailing addresses on label sheets or continuous form labels. In order to use this feature, you must have a printer that can print on labels.

1 Open the **Tools** menu and choose **Mail Merge** to display the Mail Merge Helper dialog box. Click **Create** to display a drop-down list of options. Then click **Mailing Label**. This tells Word that you are creating mailing labels.

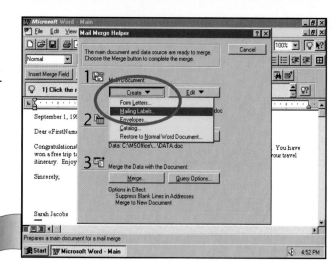

2 Word asks whether you want to change the document type or create a new main document. Click **New Main Document**. You are returned to the Mail Merge Helper dialog box to select a data source for merging.

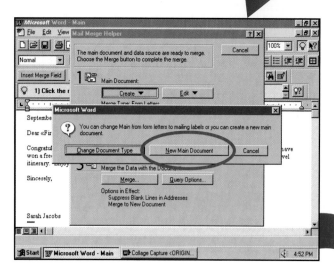

3 From the Mail Merge Helper dialog box, click **Get Data**. Then click **Open Data Source**. You see the Open Data Source dialog box.

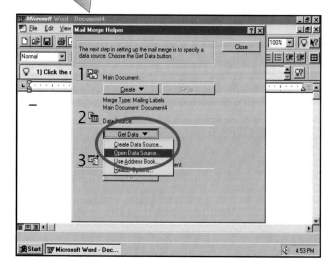

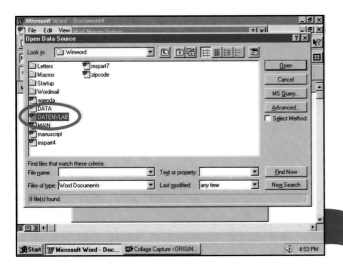

4 In the files and folders list, double-click the data source file you want to use. This tells Word to open the data file containing your address records.

5 Click **Set Up Main Document** to tell Word that you want to type in the main document.

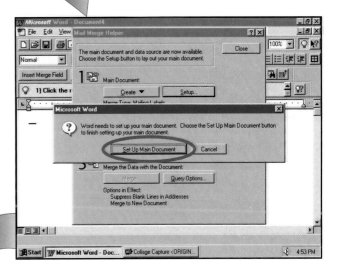

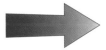

6 In the Labels Options dialog box, choose a label type from the Product Number list box. This tells Word which labels you will be using on your printer. Click **OK**.

219

7 The Create Labels dialog box appears. This is where you insert merge codes that tell Word where to insert the information for the mailing address on the label. Click the **Insert Merge Field** button. Then choose a merge field. Insert each merge field, as shown in the figure. Click **OK** and click **Close** to close the Mail Merge Helper dialog box.

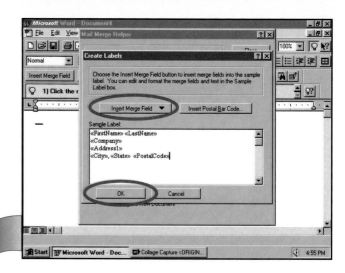

8 Type or edit the return address on the label form. Save the file and name it LABEL. Click the **Merge to Printer** button on the Mail Merge toolbar, and Word displays the Print dialog box.

9 Load the label sheets or continuous form labels in the printer. Then click **OK** to start printing addresses on the labels. ■

WHY WORRY?

If the merge didn't go as planned, check to make sure that you set up each file correctly.

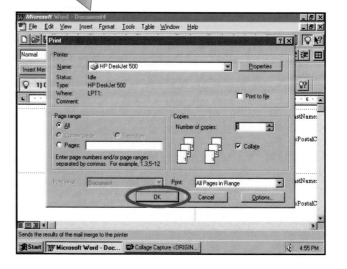

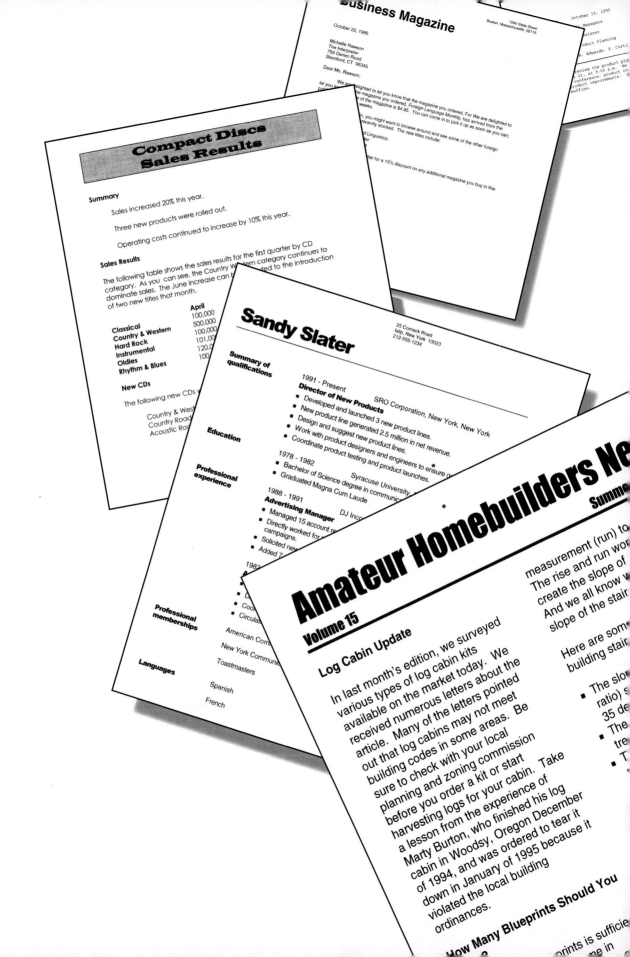

Business Magazine

October 22, 1995

Michelle Rawson
The Interpreter
750 Darien Road
Stamford, CT 06345

Dear Ms. Rawson:

We are delighted to let you know that the magazine you ordered, For We are delighted to
let you ... the magazine you ordered. *Foreign Language Monthly* has arrived from the
pub... of the magazine is $4.95. You can come in to pick it up as soon as you can;
... weeks.

... ich, you might want to browse around and see some of the other foreign
... recently stocked. The new titles include:

... d Linguistics
... er

... ter for a 15% discount on any additional magazine you buy in this

---

October 15, 1995
... Managers
... isner
... oduct Planning

... . Edwards, P. Curti...

... view the product pla...
... 21, at 9:00 a.m. We...
... conference. product ro...
... product improvements...
... muffins.

Compact Discs Sales Results

Summary

Sales increased 20% this year.

Three new products were rolled out.

Operating costs continued to increase by 10% this year.

Sales Results

The following table shows the sales results for the first quarter by CD
category. As you can see, the Country Western category continues to
dominate sales. The June increase can be ...ted to the introduction
of two new titles that month.

	April
	100,000
Classical	500,000
Country & Western	100,000
Hard Rock	101,00
Instrumental	120,0
Oldies	100,
Rhythm & Blues	

New CDs

The following new CDs ...

Country & Wes...
Country Road...
Acoustic Ro...

Sandy Slater

25 Comack Road
Islip, New York 10023
212-555-1234

Summary of qualifications

1991 - Present   SRO Corporation, New York, New York
Director of New Products
- Developed and launched 3 new product lines.
- New product line generated 2.5 million in net revenue.
- Design and suggest new product lines.
- Work with product designers and engineers to ensure q...
- Coordinate product testing and product launches.

Education

1978 - 1982
- Bachelor of Science degree in communic... Syracuse University ...
- Graduated Magna Cum Laude

Professional experience

1988 - 1991   DJ Inco...
Advertising Manager
- Managed 15 account re...
- Directly worked for...
  campaigns.
- Solicited new...
- Added 7...

198...
- D...
- Coo...
- Circular...

Professional memberships

American Com...

New York Commun...

Toastmasters...

Languages

Spanish

French

Amateur Homebuilders Ne...

Summ...

Volume 15

Log Cabin Update

In last month's edition, we surveyed
various types of log cabin kits
available on the market today. We
received numerous letters about the
article. Many of the letters pointed
out that log cabins may not meet
building codes in some areas. Be
sure to check with your local
planning and zoning commission
before you order a kit or start
harvesting logs for your cabin. Take
a lesson from the experience of
Marty Burton, who finished his log
cabin in Woodsy, Oregon December
of 1994, and was ordered to tear it
down in January of 1995 because it
violated the local building
ordinances.

measurement (run) to
The rise and run wor...
create the slope of...
And we all know w...
slope of the stair...

Here are som...
building stair...

- The slo...
  ratio) s...
  35 de...
- The...
  tre...
- T...

How Many Blueprints Should You

...prints is sufficie...
...e in...

PART X

Sample Documents

▼ Create a Memo

▼ Create a Business Letter

▼ Create a Report

▼ Create a Resumé

▼ Create a Newsletter

▼ Create an Invitation

▼ Create a Contract

▼ Create a Fax Cover Sheet

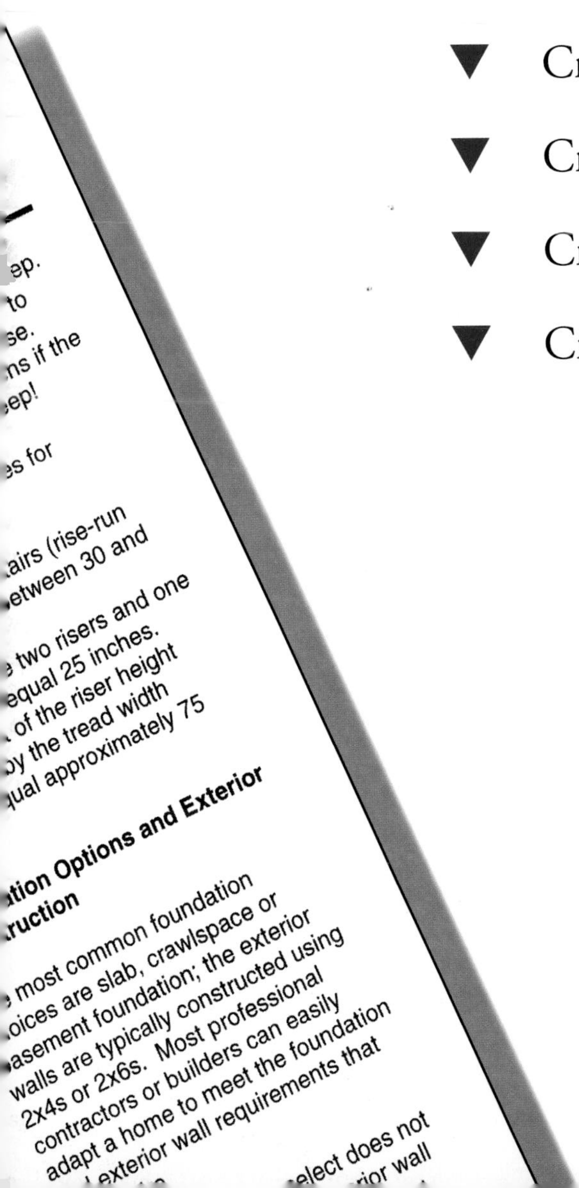

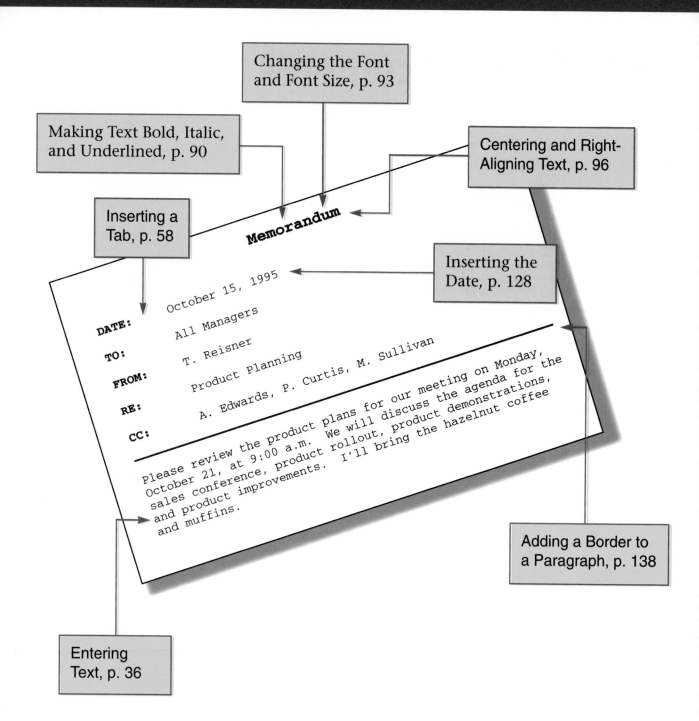

Changing the Font and Font Size, p. 93

Making Text Bold, Italic, and Underlined, p. 90

Centering and Right-Aligning Text, p. 96

Inserting a Tab, p. 58

Inserting the Date, p. 128

Memorandum

October 15, 1995

DATE:

All Managers

TO:

T. Reisner

FROM:

Product Planning

RE:

A. Edwards, P. Curtis, M. Sullivan

CC:

Please review the product plans for our meeting on Monday, October 21, at 9:00 a.m. We will discuss the agenda for the sales conference, product rollout, product demonstrations, and product improvements. I'll bring the hazelnut coffee and muffins.

Adding a Border to a Paragraph, p. 138

Entering Text, p. 36

Create a Memo

1 Change the font to Courier New 16-point. This task covers font changes:

Changing the Font and Font Size   TASK 28, p. 93

2 Type, center, and bold the heading. See these tasks for help on this step:

Centering and Right-Aligning Text   TASK 29, p. 96

Making Text Bold, Italic, and Underlined   TASK 27, p. 90

3 Change the font to Courier New 12-point. Type **TO:**, press **Tab**, and type **All Managers**. Do this for each line of the memo "address." Rather than type the date, you can insert it automatically. See these tasks:

Changing the Font and Font Size   TASK 28, p. 93

Inserting a Tab   TASK 17, p. 58

Inserting the Date   TASK 39, p. 128

4 Draw a line. This line uses the 3/4-point line style. See this task:

Adding a Border to a Paragraph   TASK 41, p. 138

5 Type the memo contents. See this task:

Entering Text   TASK 9, p. 36

6 Save and print the memo. See these tasks on saving and printing:

Saving a Document   TASK 20, p. 68

Printing the Document   TASK 55, p. 188

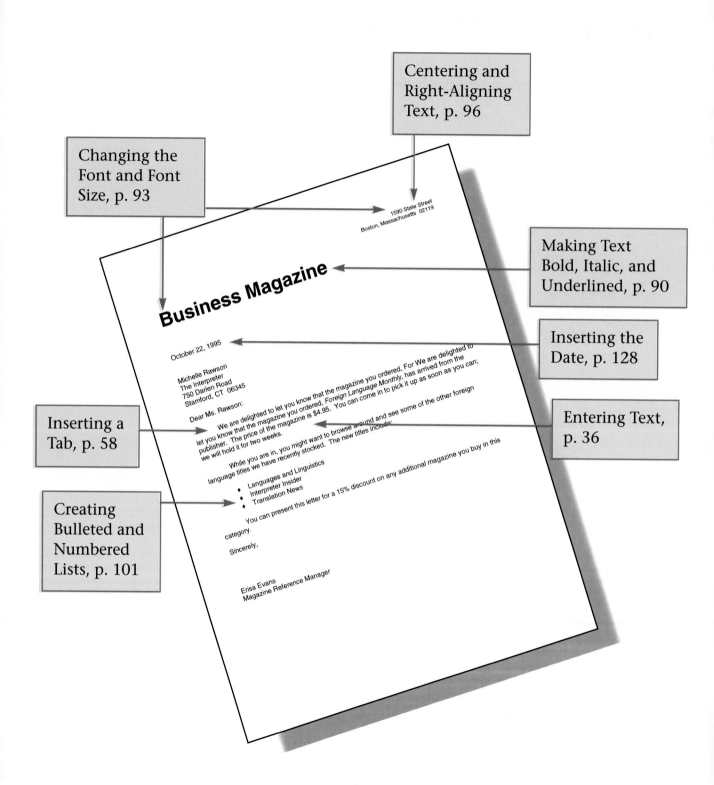

Centering and Right-Aligning Text, p. 96

Changing the Font and Font Size, p. 93

Making Text Bold, Italic, and Underlined, p. 90

Inserting the Date, p. 128

Inserting a Tab, p. 58

Entering Text, p. 36

Creating Bulleted and Numbered Lists, p. 101

1590 State Street
Boston, Massachusetts 02119

Business Magazine

October 22, 1995

Michelle Rawson
The Interpreter
750 Darien Road
Stamford, CT 06345

Dear Ms. Rawson:

We are delighted to let you know that the magazine you ordered. For We are delighted to let you know that the magazine you ordered, *Foreign Language Monthly*, has arrived from the publisher. The price of the magazine is $4.95. You can come in to pick it up as soon as you can; we will hold it for two weeks.

While you are in, you might want to browse around and see some of the other foreign language titles we have recently stocked. The new titles include:

- Languages and Linguistics
- Interpreter Insider
- Translation News

You can present this letter for a 15% discount on any additional magazine you buy in this category.

Sincerely,

Erisa Evans
Magazine Reference Manager

Create a Business Letter

1 Change the font to Arial 8-point and type the return address. Right-align the return address. See these tasks:

2 Change the font to Arial 28-point and type the company name. Bold the text. See these tasks:

3 Insert the date. This task explains how to complete this step:

4 Type the letter. The font used in this letter is Arial 10-point. You may need to italicize text. Use the Tab key to indent the paragraphs. Create the bulleted list in the letter. See these tasks:

5 Save and print the letter. See these tasks on saving and printing:

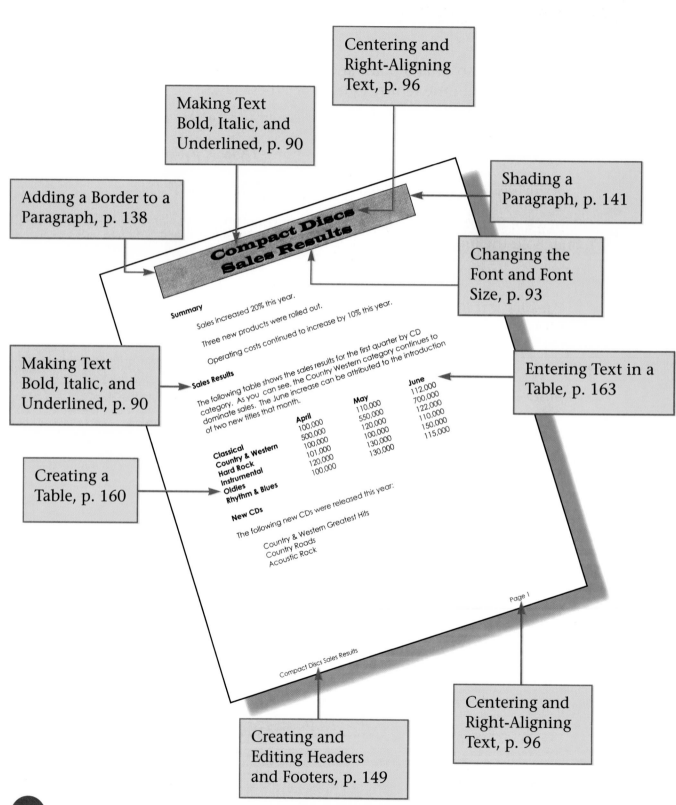

Centering and
Right-Aligning
Text, p. 96

Making Text
Bold, Italic, and
Underlined, p. 90

Shading a
Paragraph, p. 141

Adding a Border to a
Paragraph, p. 138

Changing the
Font and Font
Size, p. 93

Making Text
Bold, Italic, and
Underlined, p. 90

Entering Text in a
Table, p. 163

Creating a
Table, p. 160

Centering and
Right-Aligning
Text, p. 96

Creating and
Editing Headers
and Footers, p. 149

Create a Report

1 Type the report name. Then center it, make it bold, add a paragraph border, and add a paragraph shade. The font used is Wide Latin 18-point. These tasks cover how to apply the formatting changes:

Centering and Right-Aligning Text	*TASK 29, p. 96*
Making Text Bold, Italic, and Underlined	*TASK 27, p. 90*
Changing the Font and Font Size	*TASK 28, p. 93*
Shading a Paragraph	*TASK 42, p. 141*
Adding a Border to a Paragraph	*TASK 41, p. 138*

2 Type the report text. The text is Century Gothic 12-point type. The headings are bold. Don't forget the table! Here are the tasks to help with this step:

Entering Text	*TASK 9, p. 36*
Changing the Font and Font Size	*TASK 28, p. 93*
Making Text Bold, Italic, and Underlined	*TASK 27, p. 90*
Creating a Table	*TASK 47, p. 160*
Entering Text in a Table	*TASK 48, p. 163*

3 Add a footer with the report name and page number. The page number is right-aligned. See these tasks:

Creating and Editing Headers and Footers	*TASK 45, p. 149*
Centering and Right-Aligning Text	*TASK 29, p. 96*

4 Save and print the report. See these tasks on saving and printing:

Saving a Document	*TASK 20, p. 68*
Printing the Document	*TASK 55, p. 188*

Inserting a Tab, p. 58

Adding a Border to a Paragraph, p. 138

Changing the Font and Font Size, p. 93

Creating Bulleted and Numbered Lists, p. 101

Changing the Font and Font Size, p. 93

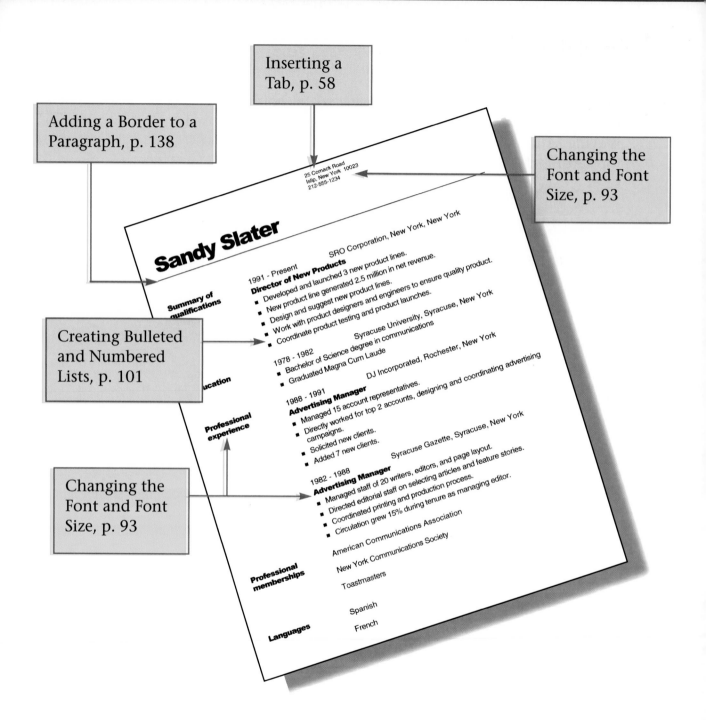

25 Comack Road
Islip, New York 10023
212-555-1234

Sandy Slater

1991 - Present SRO Corporation, New York, New York
Director of New Products

- Developed and launched 3 new product lines.
- New product line generated 2.5 million in net revenue.
- Design and suggest new product lines.
- Work with product designers and engineers to ensure quality product.
- Coordinate product testing and product launches.

1978 - 1982 Syracuse University, Syracuse, New York

- Bachelor of Science degree in communications
- Graduated Magna Cum Laude

1988 - 1991 DJ Incorporated, Rochester, New York
Advertising Manager

- Managed 15 account representatives.
- Directly worked for top 2 accounts, designing and coordinating advertising campaigns.
- Solicited new clients.
- Added 7 new clients.

1982 - 1988 Syracuse Gazette, Syracuse, New York
Advertising Manager

- Managed staff of 20 writers, editors, and page layout.
- Directed editorial staff on selecting articles and feature stories.
- Coordinated printing and production process.
- Circulation grew 15% during tenure as managing editor.

American Communications Association

New York Communications Society

Toastmasters

Spanish

French

Summary of qualifications

Education

Professional experience

Professional memberships

Languages

Create a Resumé

1 Insert a tab to indent the address and phone number. Use Arial 7-point type. See these tasks:

Changing the Font and Font Size	*TASK 28, p. 93*
Entering Text	*TASK 9, p. 36*
Inserting a Tab	*TASK 17, p. 58*

2 Type the name. The name, in this example, uses Arial MT Black 27-point type. Draw the horizontal lines. See these tasks:

Changing the Font and Font Size	*TASK 28, p. 93*
Adding a Border to a Paragraph	*TASK 41, p. 138*

3 Type the resumé. Change the font to 10-point type. Use Arial MT Black for the headings and the job titles. Create the bulleted items, as described in these tasks:

Entering Text	*TASK 9, p. 36*
Changing the Font and Font Size	*TASK 28, p. 93*
Creating Bulleted and Numbered Lists	*TASK 31, p. 101*

4 Save and print the resumé. See these tasks on saving and printing:

Saving a Document	*TASK 20, p. 68*
Printing the Document	*TASK 55, p. 188*

Centering and
Right-Aligning
Text, p. 96

Changing the
Font and Font
Size, p. 93

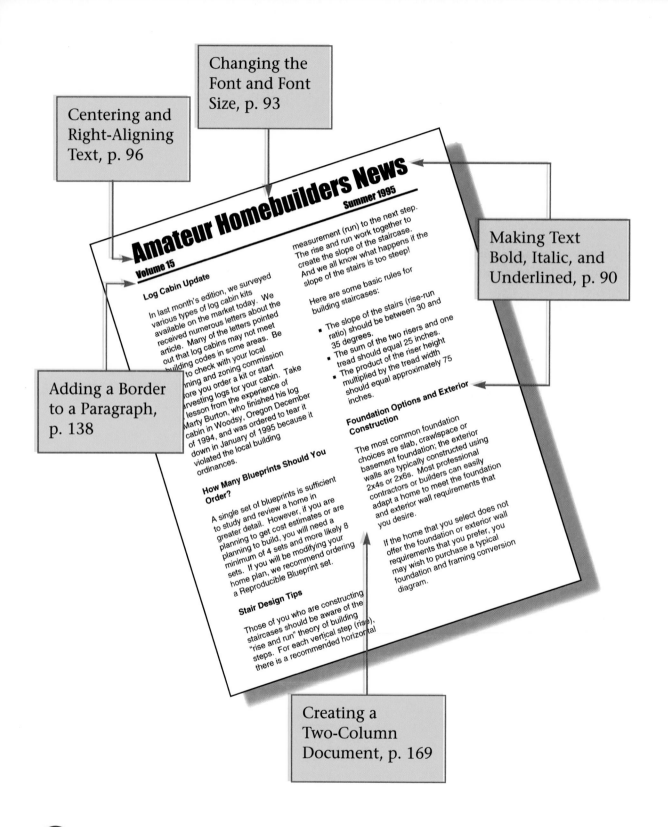

Amateur Homebuilders News

Summer 1995

Volume 15

Log Cabin Update

In last month's edition, we surveyed various types of log cabin kits available on the market today. We received numerous letters about the article. Many of the letters pointed out that log cabins may not meet building codes in some areas. Be sure to check with your local planning and zoning commission before you order a kit or start harvesting logs for your cabin. Take a lesson from the experience of Marty Burton, who finished his log cabin in Woodsy, Oregon December of 1994, and was ordered to tear it down in January of 1995 because it violated the local building ordinances.

How Many Blueprints Should You Order?

A single set of blueprints is sufficient to study and review a home in greater detail. However, if you are planning to get cost estimates or are planning to build, you will need a minimum of 4 sets and more likely 8 sets. If you will be modifying your home plan, we recommend ordering a Reproducible Blueprint set.

Stair Design Tips

Those of you who are constructing staircases should be aware of the "rise and run" theory of building steps. For each vertical step (rise), there is a recommended horizontal

measurement (run) to the next step. The rise and run work together to create the slope of the staircase. And we all know what happens if the slope of the stairs is too steep!

Here are some basic rules for building staircases:

- The slope of the stairs (rise-run ratio) should be between 30 and 35 degrees.
- The sum of the two risers and one tread should equal 25 inches.
- The product of the riser height multiplied by the tread width should equal approximately 75 inches.

Foundation Options and Exterior Construction

The most common foundation choices are slab, crawlspace or basement foundation; the exterior walls are typically constructed using 2x4s or 2x6s. Most professional contractors or builders can easily adapt a home to meet the foundation and exterior wall requirements that you desire.

If the home that you select does not offer the foundation or exterior wall requirements that you prefer, you may wish to purchase a typical foundation and framing conversion diagram.

Making Text
Bold, Italic, and
Underlined, p. 90

Adding a Border
to a Paragraph,
p. 138

Creating a
Two-Column
Document, p. 169

Create a Newsletter

1 Type the newsletter banner. The first line is centered, bold, and uses Impact 34-point type. The second line uses the same font in 14-point. See these tasks for help:

Entering Text	*TASK 9, p. 36*
Centering and Right-Aligning Text	*TASK 29, p. 96*
Making Text Bold, Italic, and Underlined	*TASK 27, p. 90*
Changing the Font and Font Size	*TASK 28, p. 93*

2 Draw a line. This line uses the 3-point line style. See this task:

Adding a Border to a Paragraph	*TASK 41, p. 138*

3 Insert a section break (continuous) and turn on two-columns. See these tasks for help:

Creating a Two-Column Document	*TASK 50, p. 169*

4 Format the headings. The headings are Arial 12-point type and bold. The article text is Arial 12-point type. See these tasks:

Changing the Font and Font Size	*TASK 28, p. 93*
Making Text Bold, Italic, and Underlined	*TASK 27, p. 90*

5 Save and print the newsletter. See these tasks on saving and printing:

Saving a Document	*TASK 20, p. 68*
Printing the Document	*TASK 55, p. 188*

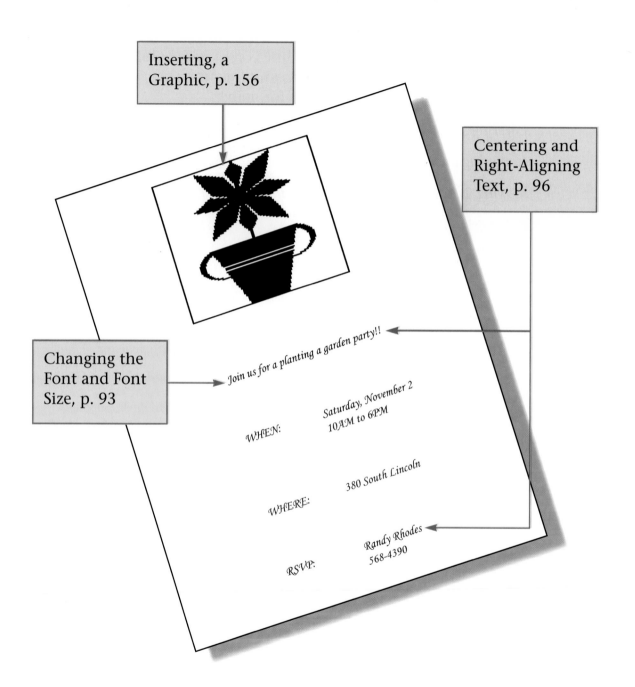

Inserting, a Graphic, p. 156

Centering and Right-Aligning Text, p. 96

Changing the Font and Font Size, p. 93

Join us for a planting a garden party!!

WHEN: Saturday, November 2
10AM to 6PM

WHERE: 380 South Lincoln

RSVP: Randy Rhodes
568-4390

Create an Invitation

1 Insert a graphic. This graphic uses the clipart FLOWER. The paragraph is centered. See this task:

Inserting a Graphic   *TASK 46, p. 156*

2 Type and center the heading. Indent the other lines with tabs. This text uses Monotype Corsiva 16-point type. See these tasks:

Entering Text   *TASK 9, p. 36*

Centering and Right-Aligning Text   *TASK 29, p. 96*

Changing the Font and Font Size   *TASK 28, p. 93*

3 Center the invitation on the page. See this task:

Centering a Page Vertically   *TASK 43, p. 144*

4 Save and print the invitation. See these tasks on saving and printing:

Saving a Document   *TASK 20, p. 68*

Printing the Document   *TASK 55, p. 188*

Making Text
Bold, Italic, and
Underlined, p. 90

Centering and
Right-Aligning
Text, p. 96

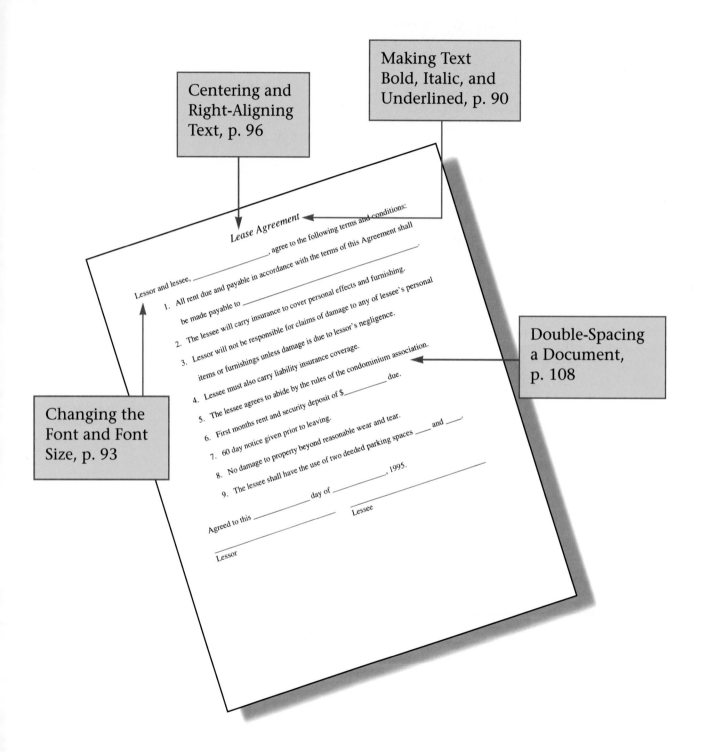

Double-Spacing
a Document,
p. 108

Changing the
Font and Font
Size, p. 93

Lease Agreement

Lessor and lessee, _____, agree to the following terms and conditions:

1. All rent due and payable in accordance with the terms of this Agreement shall be made payable to _____

2. The lessee will carry insurance to cover personal effects and furnishing.

3. Lessor will not be responsible for claims of damage to any of lessee's personal items or furnishings unless damage is due to lessor's negligence.

4. Lessee must also carry liability insurance coverage.

5. The lessee agrees to abide by the rules of the condominium association.

6. First months rent and security deposit of $_____ due.

7. 60 day notice given prior to leaving.

8. No damage to property beyond reasonable wear and tear.

9. The lessee shall have the use of two deeded parking spaces ____ and ____.

Agreed to this _____ day of _____, 1995.

_____
Lessee

_____
Lessor

Create a Contract

1 Type the heading. Make it italic and centered. This example uses Times New Roman 16-point type. See these tasks:

2 Type the contract. Create a numbered list and double-space the list. See these tasks:

3 Type a series of underscores to create the blank lines.

4 Save and print the contract. See these tasks on saving and printing:

Using a
Wizard, p. 83

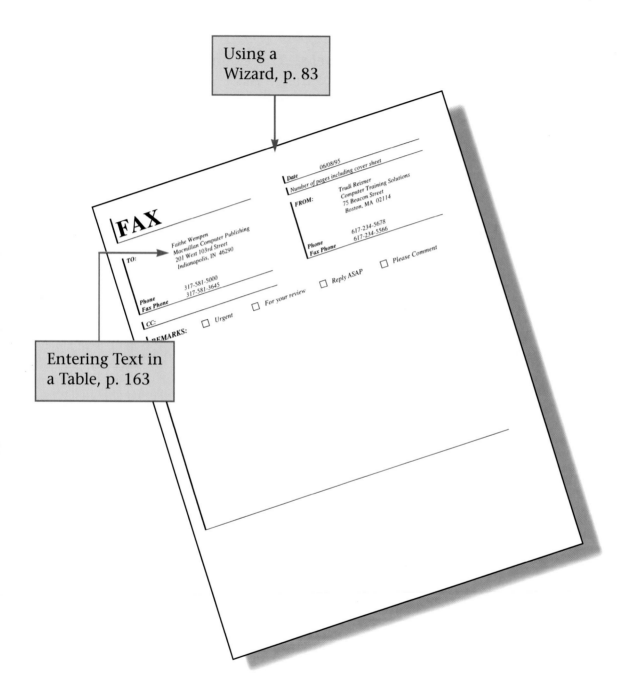

FAX

Faithe Wempen
Macmillan Computer Publishing
201 West 103rd Street
Indianapolis, IN 46290

TO:

Phone   317-581-5000
Fax Phone   317-581-3645

| Date | 06/08/95 |
| Number of pages including cover sheet | |

FROM: Trudi Reisner
Computer Training Solutions
75 Beacon Street
Boston, MA 02114

Phone   617-234-5678
Fax Phone   617-234-5566

□ Please Comment

□ Reply ASAP

□ For your review

CC: □ Urgent

REMARKS:

Entering Text in
a Table, p. 163

Create a Fax Cover Sheet

1 Use the Fax Wizard to create the fax cover sheet. Follow the instructions in each wizard dialog box. In this example, the fax cover sheet is portrait orientation and uses the contemporary style. See this task:

Using a Wizard   *TASK 26, p. 83*

2 The fax cover sheet is in a table. If you want to add any text to the table, see this task for help:

Entering Text in a Table   *TASK 48, p. 163*

3 Save and print the fax cover sheet. See these tasks on saving and printing:

Saving a Document   *TASK 20, p. 68*

Printing the Document   *TASK 55, p. 188*

Index

Symbols

PLUG YOURSELF INTO...

MACMILLAN INFORMATION SUPERLIBRARY™

que • NRP • SAMS PUBLISHING • alpha books • Hayden Books • Brady • que COLLEGE • ADOBE PRESS

THE MACMILLAN INFORMATION SUPERLIBRARY™

Free information and vast computer resources from the world's leading computer book publisher—online!

FIND THE BOOKS THAT ARE RIGHT FOR YOU!

A complete online catalog, plus sample chapters and tables of contents give you an in-depth look at *all* of our books, including hard-to-find titles. It's the best way to find the books you need!

- **STAY INFORMED** with the latest computer industry news through our online newsletter, press releases, and customized Information SuperLibrary Reports.

- **GET FAST ANSWERS** to your questions about MCP books and software.

- **VISIT** our online bookstore for the latest information and editions!

- **COMMUNICATE** with our expert authors through e-mail and conferences.

- **DOWNLOAD SOFTWARE** from the immense MCP library:
  - Source code and files from MCP books
  - The best shareware, freeware, and demos

- **DISCOVER HOT SPOTS** on other parts of the Internet.

- **WIN BOOKS** in ongoing contests and giveaways!

TO PLUG INTO MCP: →

GOPHER: gopher.mcp.com
FTP: ftp.mcp.com

WORLD WIDE WEB: **http://www.mcp.com**

Home Page • What's New • Bookstore • Reference Desk • Software Library • Macmillan Overview • Talk to Us

The easy way
to find answers

Easy Windows 95
ISBN: 1-56529-989-2
$19.99 USA
Pub Date 8/95

The *Easy* series is a full color, visual step-by-step tutorial covering over 100 common tasks and features. With screen shots for each step and a Document Gallery full of samples, this series is perfect for readers who prefer to learn visually.

Easy Excel for Windows 95
ISBN: 0-7897-0131-6
$19.99 USA
Pub Date 9/95

Easy PCs, Fourth Edition
ISBN: 0-7897-0455-2
$24.99 USA
Pub Date 9/94

Easy Internet
ISBN: 0-7897-0012-3
$24.99 USA
Pub Date 10/94

Complete and Return this Card
for a *FREE* Computer Book Catalog

Thank you for purchasing this book! You have purchased a superior computer book written expressly for your needs. To continue to provide the kind of up-to-date, pertinent coverage you've come to expect from us, we need to hear from you. Please take a minute to complete and return this self-addressed, postage-paid form. In return, we'll send you a free catalog of all our computer books on topics ranging from word processing to programming and the internet.

Mr. ☐   Mrs. ☐   Ms. ☐   Dr. ☐

Name (first) [   ]   (M.I.) ☐   (last) [   ]

Address [   ]

[   ]

City [   ]   State ☐   Zip [   ]

Phone [ ] [ ] [   ]   Fax [ ] [ ] [   ]

Company Name [   ]

E-mail address [   ]

1. Please check at least (3) influencing factors for purchasing this book.

Front or back cover information on book .... ☐
Special approach to the content .... ☐
Completeness of content .... ☐
Author's reputation .... ☐
Publisher's reputation .... ☐
Book cover design or layout .... ☐
Index or table of contents of book .... ☐
Price of book .... ☐
Special effects, graphics, illustrations .... ☐
Other (Please specify): _____ ☐

2. How did you first learn about this book?

Saw in Macmillan Computer Publishing catalog .... ☐
Recommended by store personnel .... ☐
Saw the book on bookshelf at store .... ☐
Recommended by a friend .... ☐
Received advertisement in the mail .... ☐
Saw an advertisement in: _____ ☐
Read book review in: _____ ☐
Other (Please specify): _____ ☐

3. How many computer books have you purchased in the last six months?

This book only .... ☐   3 to 5 books .... ☐
2 books .... ☐   More than 5 .... ☐

4. Where did you purchase this book?

Bookstore .... ☐
Computer Store .... ☐
Consumer Electronics Store .... ☐
Department Store .... ☐
Office Club .... ☐
Warehouse Club .... ☐
Mail Order .... ☐
Direct from Publisher .... ☐
Internet site .... ☐
Other (Please specify): _____ ☐

5. How long have you been using a computer?

☐ Less than 6 months   ☐ 6 months to a year
☐ 1 to 3 years   ☐ More than 3 years

6. What is your level of experience with personal computers and with the subject of this book?

	With PCs	With subject of book
New	☐	☐
Casual	☐	☐
Accomplished	☐	☐
Expert	☐	☐

Source Code ISBN: 0-7897-0081-6

7. Which of the following best describes your job title?

Administrative Assistant .... ☐
Coordinator .... ☐
Manager/Supervisor .... ☐
Director .... ☐
Vice President .... ☐
President/CEO/COO .... ☐
Lawyer/Doctor/Medical Professional .... ☐
Teacher/Educator/Trainer .... ☐
Engineer/Technician .... ☐
Consultant .... ☐
Not employed/Student/Retired .... ☐
Other (Please specify): _____ ☐

8. Which of the following best describes the area of the company your job title falls under?

Accounting .... ☐
Engineering .... ☐
Manufacturing .... ☐
Operations .... ☐
Marketing .... ☐
Sales .... ☐
Other (Please specify): _____ ☐

9. What is your age?

Under 20 .... ☐
21-29 .... ☐
30-39 .... ☐
40-49 .... ☐
50-59 .... ☐
60-over .... ☐

10. Are you:

Male .... ☐
Female .... ☐

11. Which computer publications do you read regularly? (Please list)

_____
_____
_____
_____
_____
_____
_____
_____
_____

Comments: _____
_____
_____

Fold here and scotch-tape to mail.

INDIANAPOLIS IN 46209-9042
201 W 103RD ST
MACMILLAN PUBLISHING USA
MACMILLAN COMPUTER PUBLISHING
ATTN MARKETING

POSTAGE WILL BE PAID BY THE ADDRESSEE

BUSINESS REPLY MAIL
FIRST-CLASS MAIL PERMIT NO. 9918 INDIANAPOLIS IN

NO POSTAGE
NECESSARY
IF MAILED
IN THE
UNITED STATES